Healing
the Vision of the
Messianic Gentile

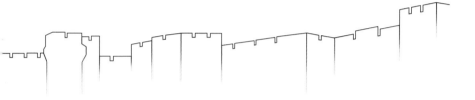

Tent
of David

BOAZ MICHAEL

Healing
the Vision of the
Messianic Gentile

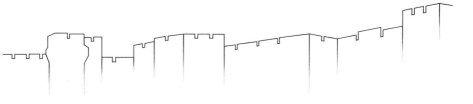

Tent

of David

BOAZ MICHAEL

First Fruits of Zion is a 501(c)(3) registered nonprofit educational organization.

First Edition 2013
Printed in the United States of America

ISBN: 978-1-892124-67-8

Scriptural quotations are from The Holy Bible, English Standard Version, copyright © 2001 by Crossway Bibles, a division of Good News Publishers. Used by permission. All rights reserved.

Design: Avner Wolff

Quantity discounts are available on bulk purchases of this book for educational, fundraising, or event purposes. Special versions or book excerpts to fit specific needs are available from First Fruits of Zion. For more information, contact www.ffoz.org/contact.

First Fruits of Zion

PO Box 649, Marshfield, Missouri 65706–0649 USA
Phone (417) 468-2741, www.ffoz.org

Comments and questions: www.ffoz.org/contact

TO MY KIDS

I will always remember the time we sang so loudly
Jason Mraz's song "I Won't Give Up" as we drove
through the Northern Galilee. We yelled, "We had
to learn how to bend without the world caving in.
I had to learn what I've got, and what I'm not and
who I am … I won't give up on us, even if the skies
get rough, I'm giving you all my love."

Thank you for all that you have given
to be a part of our mission.

Foreword

A Baptist pastor shares his heart for
the Messianic movement and its
potential to reform Christianity.

For nearly fifteen years, I have pastored a conservative evangelical Baptist congregation. For more than ten years prior, I led youth ministries in the same kinds of churches. At age seventeen, I clearly sensed God's call upon my life to serve him in the church through pastoral ministry. Seventeen years before that, I was born in a Baptist hospital! Baptist from birth. I never had a chance! Even leading up to my birth, I have a family history of ministers—my father and his father.

That's my ministry history in a nutshell; it's a not-so-interesting and rather Baptist-intensive story. I am eternally grateful for my family and for my Baptist heritage. God has used both to lead me to commit my life to Christ, to follow him with my life and to serve him through the church. However, the past eighteen months have opened up for me a more complete picture of who I am and where I came from. Through a series of circumstances, curiosity, and new friendships, I am being exposed to my Jewish roots. I have no doubt that all of these circumstances and friendships, and even my own curiosity that opened me up to the Jewish roots movement, are all God-ordained.

Through the years, I have had "glimpses" of the significance of Israel and the Jewish people. In what is now a somewhat sad memory, I recall a day in my college Old Testament Survey class. That day my thought was suddenly, "Hey! The whole Old Testament is pointing to Jesus!" What a great revelation! It is also sad that in all my upbringing in my family and church, I had never made that connection. It is also apparent that I did not know what to do with that revelation going forward.

What I realize now, after twenty-five years of ministry leadership of my own, is that the church today is still not helping to make that connection for most of the people sitting in our pews. In addition, we have treated the Hebrew Scriptures as old, outdated, and somewhat irrelevant. The very name "Old Testament" has communicated that this old part of the Scriptures has been replaced by the New Testament. We love anything that is "new and improved!" Right?

Sure, we love to quote the Ten Commandments, preach about tithing, read the beautiful poetry of the Psalms, and declare the fulfillment of the prophecies of Messiah. Yet, at the same time, the church teaches that many of God's promises and commands are no longer in effect, that the feasts and holy days commanded by God to be observed by the Jews no longer have a place, that the dietary laws are a thing of the ancient past; some teach that Christians are the new spiritual Israel and the Jewish people are no longer God's chosen people.

In all of this we struggle with the thought that the God who does not change (Numbers 23:19; 1 Samuel 15:29; James 1:17) seems to have somehow changed. My realization has been that the church today is so far removed from our Jewish roots, that very seldom do we realize that God's plan communicated through the Torah and the Jewish people has anything to do with who we are today.

All of this needs to change, and indeed, is changing. God is at work in our world and in the church reminding all of us from the nations just who he is and who his chosen people are. God is reminding us that we are the wild olive shoot grafted in to the tree of Israel. Our only connection to this tree is Messiah, and in Messiah, the only roots we have are Jewish roots.

I am convinced that in our day, God is at work revealing this in a fresh way. It is exciting and humbling all at the same time. I realize that I am not the spiritual center of my universe. Because of Jesus our Messiah, the church today stands upon God's covenants and promises which he made with Israel, not with us Gentiles. We have no covenants. The only covenants we Gentiles partake in are those made with Israel, God's chosen people.

The fact that you are reading this means you have most likely already come to this realization, have connected with your Jewish roots and have begun living out the mitzvot of God as a Messianic Gentile. In fact, many of you have clearly had a much longer experience in Jewish roots than my short eighteen months.

God has used Boaz Michael and the ministry of First Fruits of Zion to impact my life in a profound way in a very short amount of time. It is my great honor and privilege to call Boaz my friend. His passion and love for Messiah and his gentle spirit have struck a chord in our church family which has served to open many of our people to our Jewish roots, God's everlasting covenants with his people, and our place as Gentiles in God's family through our Jewish Messiah.

Boaz's desire is that this kind of loving impact will be repeated over and over again in church after church. I join with Boaz in saying, the church needs you! The church is good, yet the church needs to change. Each individual who comes to know our Jewish Messiah in his Jewish context can play a part in lovingly and patiently helping brothers and sisters in Messiah come to know him in this way as well.

God has done a work in your life. This work does not end with you. Rather, we are to become channels of God's blessings to help believers understand who they are in Messiah and to bring unbelievers to faith in him. My prayer for you is that through your experience with our Jewish Messiah, you will bless the church our Messiah so loves, for whom he died and was resurrected, and for whom he intercedes today.

Durwin Kicker
SENIOR PASTOR (MARSHFIELD FIRST BAPTIST)

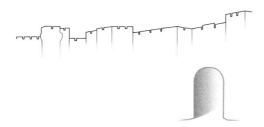

Introduction

The Church is full of potential—
but is it living up to that potential?

W e are living in an incredible, unprecedented time. An awakening is spreading across the globe. Prophecy is being
fulfilled before our eyes. Christians all over the world
are beginning to realize that there is more to their faith than they
ever thought possible—that they are partners with Israel in repair-
ing the world, spreading the gospel of the kingdom, and preparing
the way for King Messiah. They have seen their lives reinvigorated,
refreshed, and realigned by the gospel of Jesus Christ—Yeshua the
Messiah—as they reconnect with his teachings in their original
Jewish context. They are conforming their lives to his commandments in a way that would have been unthinkable and impossible
only half a century ago.

For the first time since the very early church, non-Jewish believers are actually coming into an understanding of how their lives
are to be shaped and defined by the Torah (the Mosaic Law), God's
revelation of his divine will to and for the people of Israel. To put
this in perspective, from about the fourth century to the eighteenth
century there were not even any *Jewish* believers who took on the
yoke of the Torah.[1] Today, this is changing rapidly.

For the last few hundred years, Jewish believers have been
returning to the Torah which God gave to their fathers on Mount
Sinai. This is an incredible blessing and one of the most exciting
developments in all of history—yet it should be no surprise. Based
on the Old Testament, Judaism has been teaching for millennia that
all Jews are obligated to the commandments of God, and that when
Messiah comes, he will reinforce and not abrogate the Torah. There
is also a solid basis for this renewal from Yeshua's own teachings.
The Old and New Testaments agree: the Jewish people are to remain
faithful to God's covenant through keeping the commandments of
the Torah.

The fact that Jewish believers are reengaging their own heritage represents an important part of the fulfillment of Deuteronomy 30, in which God promised the children of Israel that they would one day return to observance of the commandments which were given on Mount Sinai. This same passage contains the promise of return to the land of Israel, which we see happening even today, and the promise of a circumcised heart, which will ultimately be fulfilled through Yeshua. Jewish believers all over the world—"Messianic Jews"—are taking hold of the Sinai covenant and taking on the mitzvot (commandments) of the Torah, bringing this crucial prophecy one step closer to fulfillment.

Even more amazing, though, is the fact that non-Jewish believers are coming to the realization that they, too, have obligations to God that are shaped and defined by the very same Torah. Multitudes of Christians have discovered that there exists a very real, concrete standard by which they are required to live, and that this standard is set by the Torah.

The fact that these believers look to the Torah, the Jewish law, as a guide for their own lives is also direct fulfillment of prophecy, as the prophet Zechariah stated, "Thus says the LORD of hosts: In those days ten men from the nations of every tongue shall take hold of the robe of a Jew, saying, 'Let us go with you, for we have heard that God is with you.'"

While these believers are still Christians, for the sake of clarity and definition I will call them by the term "Messianic Gentile" (the term "Gentile" meaning nothing more than "non-Jew"). A Messianic Gentile is a non-Jewish Christian who appreciates the Torah, his relationship with Israel, and the Jewish roots of his faith.

THE NEXT STEP

Many Christians have chosen the path of the Messianic Gentile. They have seen their lives changed for the better as a result of the strides they have taken towards an understanding of their Jewish roots. They have studied, learned, and grown. At a certain point in this process of growth, though, it is not always obvious what to do next. I am frequently contacted by Messianic Gentiles who are debating what to do with their new understanding. I have connected with many communities in which this is a serious problem.

For the most part, Messianic Gentiles want to share the Messianic renewal with other believers. Grasping hold of one's Jewish roots is a wonderful thing. It is a beautiful feeling to learn about the biblical feasts, the Sabbath, and other Jewish practices which our Master embraced and taught. Our love for Yeshua makes these things precious to us. For disciples of Yeshua, finding our Jewish roots is like discovering a beautiful, long-lost treasure.

Among the many things our Master taught us was the command to love each other as he loved us (John 13:34). When we discover something beautiful, it is only natural to want to share it with the people we love. We want them to know what we know. We want them to experience the same joy, the same excitement that we have. We want them to reconnect with Yeshua in a powerful way. We want them to join the prophetic movement that God has begun among his people.

Yet this is not always easy. Churches can be resistant to the message of the Messianic Gentile. The Torah which now directs his life is the very same "Law" which most Christians believe—and have believed for centuries upon centuries—does not apply to believers at all. The message of the beauty and greatness of the Torah can be

Can one live as a Messianic Gentile among Christians
who don't yet embrace his lifestyle or viewpoint?

mistaken for legalism, the belief that one is granted eternal life on
the basis of his works.

What is the proper approach to this problem? What should the
Messianic Gentile do if he feels uncomfortable at church? How can
he communicate the joy of the Messianic life to those he cares about
without being offensive or coming off as holier-than-thou?

Can one live as a Messianic Gentile among Christians who
don't yet embrace his lifestyle or viewpoint? Is there an alternative
to church that more accurately reflects the Master's desire for his
followers?

To get answers to these questions, we must ask the apostles, as
they are the ones who initially recognized the prophetic significance
of the non-Jewish believer and who gave definition and identity to
the Messianic Gentile. The fact that such an identity exists in the
first place comes from the fact that the apostles did not require
believing Gentiles to become Jewish or to become obligated to obey
all of the Torah's commandments. Rather, the Gentiles were given
their own identity, along with a vital mission and role that is only
today being rediscovered.

This decision was made at one of the great formative moments
of Christianity, at the Jerusalem Council. And as much as it is taken
for granted today that Christians are not required to become Jewish,
this was actually an incredibly controversial position in the early
church. Nevertheless, it is the position that prevailed. In Acts 15, the
apostles decided to limit the obligations of Gentile believers and not

to lay on them the requirement to be circumcised and become Jewish. If they had not done this, all believers today would have to be Jewish or proselytes to Judaism. There is really no way to overestimate how influential and formative this decision was.

Many years later, as recorded in Acts 21, the apostles reaffirmed that the Jewish believers in Jerusalem were all "zealous for the Law." To clarify the key difference between Jewish and Gentile believers, they continued: "But as for the Gentiles who have believed, we have sent a letter with our judgment that they should abstain from what has been sacrificed to idols, and from blood, and from what has been strangled, and from sexual immorality" (Acts 21:25).

Based on this ruling and on the revelation Christ gave to him personally, the apostle Paul staunchly fought for the right of Gentile believers to remain Gentiles. This is actually what Paul was arguing for in Galatians 3:28: "There is neither Jew nor Greek, there is neither slave nor free, there is no male and female, for you are all one in Christ Jesus." In other words, the body of Messiah accepts everyone as they are—it doesn't matter whether you're slave or free, male or female, Jew or Gentile. You don't have to become something you're not in order to follow Yeshua.

TENT OF DAVID

But why? Why was it so important that Gentile believers remain Gentiles and not become Jews? After all, the Jewish people had been the locus of God's activity on earth for, at that time, two thousand years. Why were the apostles so adamant that Gentiles retain their identity as Gentiles? It turns out that the return of the Gentiles under the rule of King Messiah was an important prophetic development, one in which believers today are still taking part. These

Gentiles were a vital and necessary part of what God was going to accomplish in the world.

At the Jerusalem Council, when James and the apostles were discussing the role of the Gentiles who were coming to faith in Yeshua, James quoted Amos 9:11-12: "'After this I will return, and I will rebuild the tent of David that has fallen; I will rebuild its ruins, and I will restore it, that the remnant of mankind may seek the Lord, and all the Gentiles who are called by my name,' says the Lord, who makes these things known from of old" (Acts 15:16-18).

The Tent of David is a reference to the Davidic kingdom, which Amos envisions will encompass even the Gentiles, non-Jews who attach themselves to Israel and to Israel's Messiah. James reckoned that the believing Gentiles of his day were the first fruits of the fulfillment of Amos' prophecy.

The concept of the Tent of David, central as it is to the identity of the church and the Messianic Gentile, is seriously underappreciated. The prophets envisioned a kingdom that brought myriads of Gentiles to the knowledge of the Messiah and submission to his rule. Isaiah (2:2) prophesied that people from all nations—Gentiles—would flow to Jerusalem and worship there. Later in Isaiah (11:10-12), Messiah is said to inspire Gentiles to come to him as well as regather the scattered Jewish people. Isaiah 49:6; Micah 4:2; and Zechariah 8:22-23 contain similar prophecies.

The Lord's brother saw the potential and the prophetic necessity for Yeshua-believing Gentiles and Jews to partner in making the prophets' vision a reality. The Messiah had come and Gentiles were coming to him in droves. Paul's ministry was devoted to making the "obedience of faith" a reality in the Gentile community, connecting his Gentile believers to Israel and teaching them how to properly submit to the rule of King Messiah.[2]

The Gentile believers, as part of this commonwealth,
had a unique and vital role in the process of building
the Tent of David, using their numbers and resources to
empower and bless the Jewish community and spread
the message of the kingdom in their own culture.

The apostles desired that Gentile believers would partner with the believing Jewish community, begin practicing what would have then been considered a form of Judaism in solidarity with the Jewish people, live a life of submission to the Messiah King, and work alongside Messianic Jews to spread the message of the kingdom throughout the nations. The apostle Paul called the resulting alliance between believing Jew and Gentile the "commonwealth of Israel" (Ephesians 2:12).

The Gentile believers, as part of this commonwealth, had a unique and vital role in the process of building the Tent of David, using their numbers and resources to empower and bless the Jewish community and spread the message of the kingdom in their own culture. In this way, the apostles envisioned the imminent restoration of the Tent of David and the establishment of Yeshua's hegemony over the entire world. This apocalyptic-eschatological vision was really the defining impetus of the apostles' entire Gentile mission. It would hardly be an overstatement to say that this apostolic vision is Christianity's *raison d'être*, its reason for existing.

Two thousand years later, two billion people profess to believe in Yeshua. By any measure, this is a victory. Yet in some ways, this victory rings hollow. How many of these believers really see Yeshua as a Jew, and King of the Jews? How many recognize the continuing role of Israel and the Torah in God's plan? Can the Tent of David truly be restored if there is no connection between the historical people of God (the Jewish people) and the Gentiles who attach themselves to God? And most importantly, how many Christians have taken on the mission the apostles gave them? How many are really living the Messianic ideal, truly and wholeheartedly dedicating their lives to following the teachings of Yeshua and spreading his message far and wide—establishing and expanding the Tent of David?

This book is inspired by Stuart Dauermann's *Son of David: Healing the Vision of the Messianic Jewish Movement*.[3] In it, he described the Messianic Jewish congregational movement and the church as "two blind men still needing to be healed."[4] Dauermann focused on what he perceived to be the core problem of the Messianic Jewish movement: its failure to recognize and prioritize Yeshua's role as the Son of David, the great King, and the ramifications of this fact for Messianic Jews. He also concerns himself throughout with the low view of Jewish life and Torah faithfulness among Messianic Jews in the Messianic Jewish congregational movement.

Dauermann mentioned in passing the church's blind spot as well—the Jewishness of Yeshua. And while Messianic Jews have their work cut out for them as they contemplate the correction Dauermann has tried to bring, in reading *Son of David* I felt that Messianic Gentiles needed a cognate work. Messianic Gentiles are on the cutting edge of one of the most important and unprecedented revivals in history. To that end, they have expended immeasurable energy trying to restore an apostolic form of worship, and rightly so. However, their purpose and role in God's plan is far bigger than that—and at the same time, it is right on their doorstep: hundreds of thousands of churches are waiting for someone to show them

Yeshua's Jewishness and help then to reconnect with their prophetic mission.

To fully rebuild the Tent of David and see the apostolic vision restored, we must help the mainstream church—the historical venue for Christ-belief—to recognize Yeshua as a Torah-observant Jew and eternal King of the Jews, which entails the acceptance of the Jewish people as God's chosen people and the acceptance of Torah observance as God's continuing covenantal requirement for the Jewish people. *More than that*, we must light a fire of passion in the hearts of our fellow Christians, a fire that drives them to reconnect with Yeshua as their rabbi in a way they have never experienced before, and to spread the message of the kingdom far and wide.

RESTORING THE VISION OF THE MESSIANIC GENTILE

As disciples of the Messiah, Messianic Gentiles must live out by personal example the teachings of Yeshua and demonstrate vividly to mainstream Christians what it means to be an enthusiastic, totally devoted disciple of Rabbi Yeshua. As those who have truly encountered the living Jewish Yeshua, it is their responsibility to show him to the broader Christian world. This calling is uniquely suited to Messianic Gentiles, who are familiar with the culture around them, speak the language, and can easily build solidarity with members of the nations. In this way, they help bring the apostles' vision to fruition.

The prophets envisioned an eschatological scenario in which Gentiles, members of the nations, join together with Israel and worship the God of Israel together—yet retaining their distinctive roles. This prophetic vision requires both Jew and Gentile to apprehend and live out their unique role and calling.

R. Kendall Soulen wrote:

> Apart from Israel, Gentiles would not exist. Upon consideration, this is not hyperbolic speech but a sober statement of theological reality. A Gentile is by definition a non-Jew. At a semantic level, therefore, there could be no Gentiles without Jews. This linguistic reality points to a more basic theological truth. The Lord's election of Israel is a situation-creating reality that determines the existence and identity not only of Israel, but also of the rest of human creation. Gentile identity is a category of covenant history just as certainly and irrevocably as is Jewish identity. To be a Gentile *means* to be the other of Israel and as such a full participant in a single economy of mutual blessing anchored in God's carnal election of the Jewish people.[5]

The original role and calling of the non-Jewish Christian, then, is a member of the nations who cleaves to the Messiah of Israel and participates in God's blessings along with the Jewish people, as part of the commonwealth of Israel. Ideally, as many Gentiles as possible will participate in this "economy of mutual blessing," understanding that they are blessed by God but that these blessings (and particularly the knowledge of God) are mediated through the Jewish people in general and through King Messiah in particular.

As it stands, most Christians do not have a full understanding of the role of the Jewish people or of the Torah in God's process of consummation and redemption. This roadblock is keeping the Tent of David from being restored. The Tent needs both Jews and Gentiles to accept and live out their respective callings. If Gentile believers—Christians—don't do their part, if they don't recognize their connection with the Jewish people and their particular role in the commonwealth of Israel, then the apostles' vision will never see the light of day.

Who will show the institutional church its blind spot? Who will work to restore the apostolic vision to the followers of Yeshua? The Messianic Gentile is the most likely person God can use to bring the message of Yeshua's Jewishness and the continuing role of Israel and the Torah to the believing members of the nations—that is, to other Christians.

This is the great mission of the Messianic Gentile: to be that voice *within the church* that speaks gently but firmly against supersessionism and the doctrinal errors associated with it; that speaks toward the church's connection with the land, the people, and the scriptures of Israel; that inspires people to connect with Yeshua in a new and fresh way and to follow his teachings with unprecedented zeal. In this way, by sharing what they have discovered with other Christians, Messianic Gentiles can play an essential, active, key role in restoring the apostolic vision.

This can only happen, though, if those Christians who understand their Jewish roots choose to remain in their churches as faithful congregants.

This means that in order to take on this mission, Messianic Gentiles must remain involved with the churches to which they have already committed themselves. They must maintain a positive relationship with their brothers and sisters in Christ, as practicing and participating members within their church community. They must continue to pursue healthy relationships with their fellow believers and be a living example of what it means to follow Yeshua the Jewish Messiah.

PERSONAL TESTIMONY

I can testify to the importance of this mission personally—I am living it out. Much of this book is a result of my intentions and effort. I am a Messianic Jew. My great grandmother was the last one in our family to care enough about Jewish identity that she requested to be buried in a Jewish cemetery. That seemed to be the last breath of Jewish heritage in my family. Faith or even belief in God was lost in subsequent generations as everyone assimilated into mainstream American secular culture.

My parents came to faith as a result of a faithful Christian knocking on their apartment door, sharing the gospel message and reconciling them back to God. Years later, in my early youth, we were compelled to reconnect to Messianic Judaism by another faithful servant who came into the church to share Jewish perspectives on our faith. These two servants are part of my spiritual heritage.

In my early twenties, I formally reconciled my Jewishness back to the Jewish people through a conversion. While I was studying with an Orthodox rabbi, he, seeing my zeal and knowing my family history, offered to take me through a conversion without forcing me to renounce my faith in Messiah. Perceiving this as a door opened by God, I walked through it.

This formal reconnection with the Jewish people is something my family is now defined by. I have family living in Israel, I have children in the IDF (Israeli Defense Forces), and I live a life consistent with traditional Judaism. Some Jews do not accept me because of my faith in Yeshua—I understand and accept that. However, I cannot escape the sense that my life is ordered by the Lord and that he orchestrated events and people in my life to make me who I am today.

My situation is really no different from that of Timothy. Timothy's parents were a mixed marriage (a Greek father and a Jewish mother), and they must have been Hellenized on some level, as they did not care enough about Judaism (or Torah) to have Timothy circumcised. Thus Paul had him circumcised as an adult to be able to be recognized amongst the people of Israel. However, Titus, being a Gentile, was not circumcised by Paul, as an example of God considering the believing members of the nations clean and partners with Israel without having to become Jewish.

Though I was brought to faith in a Christian context, today I identify primarily as a Jew practicing Judaism and not as a Christian. I, like many others, am part of the emerging Messianic Jewish movement. I feel that my proper place of worship is a Messianic synagogue; if there were one close to where I live, I would attend. Yet I have chosen to invest my time and energy at a local Baptist church. I support this church and attend services every week that I am able. Even if there were a Messianic synagogue nearby, I would still make the sacrifice to connect to the local church because I believe in the mission to bring reformation and change, and to help establish the church's connection to Israel.

I have gotten to know the pastor and the people there and have found them to be devoted, God-fearing believers. In turn, because I respect and affirm what they are doing, they have begun to respect my point of view. I meet with the pastor weekly, and I can tell that even in the short time I have been involved with that church, the atmosphere has changed. More and more, the sermons reflect a theology that has rejected supersessionism. Additionally, I have not had to curtail my level of observance one iota—I remain a fully observant Jew.

A SENSE OF MISSION

I have taken this mission seriously. And though I may have had an advantage as a known quantity, the director of an international publishing ministry, it has also been the experience of many others that if Messianic Gentiles would remain in the church as faithful congregants who support the mission and vision of the church both ideologically and financially, there is a high degree of probability that they will eventually be given an opportunity to help bring this vital message of hope and renewal to their friends and loved ones in the church.

More than that, if Messianic Gentiles can really grasp the significance of the kingship of Yeshua the Jewish Messiah and the urgency of the task of following him completely, their excitement and zeal will inevitably be contagious. People around them—Christian or not—will want to attach themselves to the Messiah as they see the *gemilut chasadim*, the "kind deeds," of his followers.

Messianic Gentiles have the potential to impact and inform hundreds of thousands—perhaps millions of Christians who would immediately be sympathetic to our cause, if only the message were presented in the right way. After all, committed Christians *want* to know Yeshua better. They want to understand and follow his teachings. They want others to inspire them and help keep them accountable in their spiritual growth.

The core message of the Jewish roots of the Christian faith is completely biblical and it is supported by modern scholarship. It is good and necessary and has the potential to radically reform Christianity. But this will only happen if many of those who take hold of this message remain in the church and become advocates for it at both the congregational and the denominational level.

To some, this mission looks impossible due to its sheer scope; we are, after all, trying to reach the entire Christian world—and beyond. To complicate matters, because of the insights they have gained through their reconnection with their Jewish roots, some Messianic Gentiles may no longer agree with all of the church's traditional doctrinal stances (particularly concerning Israel and the Torah). Attending a church with which one doesn't fully agree can be difficult. It requires sacrifice and humility. It requires patience and loving kindness. But ultimately, in spite of the difficulty, I believe this is one of the most important missions the Father has for Messianic Gentiles, and that vast numbers of them are urgently being called to it—prophetically, it is vital.

I know that some will object to the idea that Messianic Gentiles should remain in the churches to which they have previously committed. To be sure, this mission is not for everyone. It will take a special kind of person to do this job well. We are not encouraging those Messianic Gentiles who have already found homes in established Messianic congregations to leave their fellowships behind. Neither is this book intended to encourage a mass exodus of Messianic Gentiles from the Messianic Jewish movement. That is not the point of this book. The Messianic Jewish movement[6] needs those of the nations to join with her, help establish Messianic Judaism as a viable, sustainable movement, and rebuild what was lost—provided that this cooperation is undertaken with care, love, and the utmost respect for the synagogue's leadership and the vision of its congregation.

Rather, this book is for those believers who grew up or began a relationship with Yeshua in a Christian context, who have since grasped hold of their Jewish roots, and who are seeking to share and expand their newfound understanding. I have had the honor of connecting with many U.S.-based and international communities of

I know that some will object to the idea that
Messianic Gentiles should remain in the churches
to which they have previously committed. To
be sure, this mission is not for everyone.

Messianic Jewish and Gentile believers. I have counseled individuals, pastors, and families about "what to do" with their new Messianic understanding of the Bible. I have heard the concerns of many about the need for the church to change. This book is intended to encourage Messianic Gentiles to begin putting forth the effort and sacrifice to effect this needed change. It is my deep passion to bring restoration to the church and see it become a positive reflection of the God of Israel. Yet it will require hard and continuous work.

In this book, I hope to deal with some objections to this vision and to outline a broad strategy for helping Christian churches to reconnect with their roots. Chapter one is a brief overview of what is good in Christianity, including the mitzvot of the Torah that almost all Christians already keep, and the modern Evangelical movement's awareness of its connection with Israel. Chapter two details some of the relevant problems in Christian doctrine, including the problem of supersessionism and Christianity's historically low view of the Torah and the Jewish people, as well as proposed alternatives to these viewpoints shaped by modern Christian scholarship.

Chapter three introduces the concept of the *shaliach*, the "ambassador" for the Messiah, and some of the steps necessary to cultivate that ideal in one's personal life. Chapter four investigates the broader context of the mission and the ethical issues involved. Chapter five discusses what it takes to tactfully and appropriately reintroduce one's fellow Christians to their Jewish Messiah. Chapter six condenses the mission of the *shaliach* into a formal strategic plan with identifiable and measurable goals. Appendix A introduces the *shaliach* to the different denominations of Christianity and the unique challenges and opportunities they present. Appendix B lists some important and useful resources that will aid the *shaliach* in his mission.

It is my sincere hope and prayer that together, we can accomplish something great, something unprecedented and wonderful for the kingdom, and bring great honor to the name of our Messiah. We can help restore the Tent of David, but it won't be easy. It will take serious thought, prayer, research, and dedication. It will take humility, grace, self-understanding, and love. It will take a move of the Spirit in our hearts and in the hearts of those that we encounter.

Yet we are sure to succeed. The entire scope of the prophetic literature of the Old Testament looks forward to our day, to the time when the nations begin to rally around Israel and support her in her mission to show the God of Abraham to the entire world. The fact that the Messianic movement exists at all is evidence that the fulfillment of that prophecy is at hand. The apostles' vision is finally coming to fruition. After two long millennia, we are privileged to witness and take part in this amazing, prophetic renewal.

The coming renewal is going to strengthen the church. It is going to be a revival the likes of which it has never seen before. It is going to return to the church something it lost long ago—its original, apostolic mission and its relationship to the Jewish people. The renewed, strengthened church will then, in turn, strengthen Israel, as the church comes alongside her to encourage and support her in her God-given mission.

Everyone in life needs a sense of mission, an attachment to something of greater importance, the answer to the question, "Why am I here?" My hope for this book is that those godly and sincere Christians who have connected to the God of Israel will capture a glimpse of their mission, put their hand to the plow, and transform their world.

> You are not required to complete the task, you are not free to withdraw from it ... but be aware that the reward of the righteous will be given in the World to Come. (*Pirkei Avot* 2:21)

The Church Is Good

The church has been the locus of God's
activity among non-Jews for thousands of
years. In that time, it has done much good.

To most Christians, the title of this chapter will sound nearly ridiculous in its self-evidence. Yet I think it is important, when seeking to bring correction, to place that correction in the context of affirmation. I am not trying to tear the church down, God forbid. My desire is to strengthen the church and to help it fulfill the mission given it by the apostles. I believe the church is fundamentally good and that it has the potential to accomplish that mission.

In this chapter and the next I hope to help Messianic Gentiles and those who have recently been exposed to the Messianic movement to take a step back and honestly appraise Christianity. It is my position that at its core, Christianity is good. The church is good.[7] Nobody is perfect, and the institutional church has, throughout history, made mistakes—we'll go over them in the next chapter. But first, we must be sure to understand that Christianity is a move of God, full of genuine, Spirit-filled believers who have done amazing, miraculous things for the kingdom of God.

Yet even before delving into an appraisal of the institutional church, it is important to recognize the common ground on which we stand. By any biblical definition, all believers in Yeshua the Messiah are part of one body, the *ecclesia* of God. All who have made Yeshua their master are subjects of one kingdom, the kingdom of heaven.

I believe the term "Messianic" is an easy-to-understand descriptor that helps Christians who understand their Jewish roots to find a concrete identity and definition. Yet to be a "Messianic Gentile" does not make one something other than a "Christian."

"Christian" and "Messianic" are absolute synonyms, one from a Greek root and the other from a Hebrew root, both meaning "to anoint." They both refer to the same Messiah, and though they may have different connotations in our culture, the first believers would have regarded them as interchangeable.

As a Messianic Jew, I am a Jewish follower of the Jewish Messiah; Gentile believers have also attached themselves to the same Messiah. So we are all Christians according to the word's original, lexical meaning—Christ-followers. God forbid that the term "Messianic" should foster an "us vs. them" mentality toward Christians who do not accept the Messianic viewpoint; this attitude is counterproductive, unbiblical, and unnecessary.

SIMPLE MESSAGE—SIMPLY BEAUTIFUL

A common complaint against modern evangelical Christianity is that it emphasizes the simple gospel message of salvation through faith in Yeshua the Messiah, almost to the exclusion of all other aspects of doctrine and practice.

In one sense, this complaint is justified, as we will discuss below. However, the basic Christian message—that one can have their sins forgiven and gain a place in the World to Come by believing in Yeshua—is true and absolutely biblical. God has chosen to save people who believe in Yeshua, even though they don't deserve it.

Recall the thief on the cross. His story was undoubtedly included in the gospel message because it is so iconic for the vast majority of believers, who will never understand or apprehend any more complicated doctrine than the simple message of salvation through Yeshua. Like so many of those Yeshua touched during his life, the thief's faith made him whole. His entire life of crime was forgotten and he was promised a place in Paradise.

It is tempting to think this message is too simple—that because of its simplicity, it must be fundamentally wrong or a misunderstanding of the Bible's teaching. Yet like the thief on the cross, simple people who have taken the step of putting their faith in Yeshua can expect to be given a place in the World to Come.

This idea lies at the heart of the gospel message. Yeshua doesn't save people because of what they have done—if it were so, none of us would merit salvation. Yeshua saves people because of what he did.

It is not anyone's place to pass judgment on those who are infants in their faith, who have not taken on this or that mitzvah. James wrote in his epistle (4:11–12), "Do not speak evil against one another, brothers. The one who speaks against a brother or judges his brother, speaks evil against the law and judges the law. But if you judge the law, you are not a doer of the law but a judge. There is only one lawgiver and judge, he who is able to save and to destroy. But who are you to judge your neighbor?"

In essence, this passage communicates to us that the pace of someone else's spiritual development is God's concern alone (though God did empower the community to take action in certain situations—see for example 1 Corinthians 5). God has not appointed us to judge someone else based on his or her level of observance; to do so is tantamount to judging the law itself. James even goes so far as to say that one who judges another's level of observance has ceased to observe the Torah himself. God alone is able to judge—and also able to save.

The simplicity of the gospel represents the strength and beauty of the work of Yeshua, who has the power to save sinners—and we have, all of us, sinned. As the Messianic Gentile grows in his understanding, he must be careful not to judge other Christians' destinies or the state of their hearts based on their failure to observe mitzvot or apprehend deep, complex concepts.

Nevertheless, the reduction of the gospel to *nothing more than belief*, to the idea that one can live whatever kind of life one wants and still claim to be "saved," is an abuse of the gospel message and has resulted in untold harm. This unfortunate fallacy will be addressed in the next chapter, where we explore the idea that the gospel is far more than just the message of personal salvation.

UNDESERVED CRITICISM: PAGANISM

Probably the most serious accusation that believers have leveled against institutional Christianity in recent years is that it is rooted in paganism rather than Judaism.[8] The practices and even the theology of mainstream Christianity have all been called into question, even by Christian leaders and teachers. Christmas, Easter, Sunday worship, the design of church buildings, the role of the pastor, and many more hallmarks of Christianity have been analyzed and rejected on the basis that they derive solely from pagan philosophy and pagan practices.

Popular Christian authors Frank Viola and George Barna compiled many of these concerns in their book *Pagan Christianity?*,[9] an unflattering exploration of the supposed roots of many Christian practices. The book reads like an exposé; one would think, reading Viola, that nearly everything that characterizes modern Christian worship is unbiblical—and, by extension, wrong. Criticizing everything from the seating to the music to the pulpit, Viola advocates a total revolution back to what he calls the "organic church," with no hierarchical leadership, no church building, and no sermon. This, to Viola, mirrors the practice of the early church.

Viola's concerns are not totally without merit. Some of the functional developments of the church have made it more difficult to implement the New Testament's teaching. Yet his greatest error is his failure to recognize the Jewish roots of Christianity.[10] Using only a few scattered New Testament texts and ignoring the historical evidence of Christianity's origins in liturgical Jewish synagogue worship, Viola paints an idealistic picture in which all Christians meet in small home groups and conduct impromptu, disorganized worship services. Later developments, he claims, came from paganism, but traditions which Christianity borrowed or adapted from the synagogue—having a defined place of worship, for instance—can certainly not be called "pagan." One wonders how out of place Viola would have felt in the formal and structured synagogue in Nazareth, listening to Yeshua's *drash* on Isaiah 61, in the midst of a liturgical prayer service.

In his study "What about Paganism?" Toby Janicki addressed some of the outlandish claims that have been made about the supposed pagan origins of Christian practices. As it turns out, many of these claims have their roots in an infamous nineteenth-century work called *The Two Babylons* by Alexander Hislop. This anti-Catholic treatise has long been recognized as a work of fiction, full of errors and falsehood and based on bad scholarship.

Janicki's study reveals that many of the myths regarding the supposed pagan origins of Easter, Christmas, Sunday worship, and other Christian practices are blown out of proportion. It is true that as Christian praxis developed, it took on traditions that were not explicitly Jewish and even appropriated practices from paganism. In time, specifically Jewish practices were even discouraged and eliminated. However, even though Christianity did unfortunately adopt some practices that resemble pagan rites, the result was not idol worship. It was a form of worship based essentially on Judaism that was culturally appropriate and accessible for the Gentile believers who espoused it.

Yes, it is sad that Passover was swallowed up by a de-Judaized holiday which we now know as Easter (yet still called *Pascha* or some derivative thereof in most languages) in the early church. But that doesn't make the celebration of the resurrected Messiah through the platform of an Easter service a pagan festival. Hislop's pseudo-scholarly derivation of Easter from ancient Babylonian worship is patently false; the term "Easter" is not derived from the Semitic "Ishtar" but from the Germanic goddess Ēostre, which lent its name not directly to the Christian festival, but to the month in which it fell. The name's pagan significance is no greater than that of the month of March, which is named for Mars, the Roman god of war. While the name change from Pesach to Easter is unfortunate and inappropriate, it does not reflect a Babylonian origin.

When devout Christians celebrate Easter, they think only of the resurrection of Yeshua the Messiah. And while there are many distractions that take away from the proper focus and intention of the holiday, many Christians understand how problematic the pagan-derived imagery is (eggs, rabbits, etc.) and choose not to include it in their celebration.

In the proper sense of the term, there is no *inherent* idol-worship in the Resurrection celebration. In fact, Easter is one of the easiest teaching tools available to a Messianic Gentile who desires to bring his brothers and sisters to a better knowledge of Yeshua's Jewishness. On years in which the two holidays fall in close proximity, attending a Passover celebration or seder meal in connection with Holy Week can be a powerful learning experience for traditional Christians interested in reliving Yeshua's last week.

Similarly, Sunday worship originated as a weekly remembrance of the resurrection. It has its origins in the second century at the latest, and perhaps earlier, placing it within decades of the apostles themselves, if not in their lifetimes. It has no connection with worship of the sun, or Mithra, nor does it have any other pagan connotation. The myth of Constantine's institution of Sunday worship in the fourth century has even been abandoned by its chief propagator, the Seventh Day Adventist church, which now places the origin of Sunday worship in the early second century based on the research of Samuele Bacchiocchi.[11]

Instead of focusing on the negative—that Christianity has lost the biblical observances of Passover and Sabbath—we ought to remember the positive: that several billion people, a significant part of the entire world population, remember weekly and yearly the death and resurrection of the King of the Jews. That the name of Yeshua would be honored in every place, and that people all over the world would be drawn to him, is a fulfillment of biblical prophecy (Luke 2:32; Isaiah 11:10, 42:6, 49:6; Philippians 2:9–11; John 12:32). This is something to rejoice about, not condemn.

In this light, how much more fruitful will our efforts be if we are careful to emphasize to other Christians their connection with Yeshua through the Passover, Sabbath, and other mitzvot, instead of wasting our time, our energy, and our reputations by denigrating Christian customs? Consider how easy it would be to completely turn off a traditional Christian to the message of Yeshua's Jewishness by inadvertently insulting and degrading his religion. This would surely cause the substance, meaning, and beauty of the mitzvot to be obscured.

UNDESERVED CRITICISM: ANTINOMIANISM

Another term I have heard used to refer to mainstream Christianity is "antinomian." The word "antinomian" (coined by a devout Christian, Martin Luther[12]) comes from the Greek word *nomos* (law) and the prefix *anti* (against). Because nomos is a Greek cognate to the Hebrew "Torah," one might think "antinomian" is a clever way of

Instead of focusing on the negative, we ought to remember the positive: that several billion people ... remember weekly and yearly the death and resurrection of the King of the Jews.

saying "anti-Torah"—as in, "Most Christians don't keep the Torah's dietary laws, so they must be antinomian."

While the rediscovery of the Torah's eternal significance and relevance is positive, the charge of antinomianism is absolutely the least productive way to bring other people to this realization. This is true for several reasons.

First, the word antinomian, in its normal Christian context (the context in which it originated), refers to someone who has thrown off any inhibitions whatsoever. Paul often spoke against this kind of moral license, especially in connection with the doctrine of justification by faith (Romans 3:8; all of chapter 6; Galatians 5:13–26; 1 Corinthians 6:9–20; and many other passages). Luther's coinage of the term originated in similar circumstances, as his emphasis on the doctrine of justification by faith was interpreted by some as a license to sin.

The term "antinomian" is then extremely inappropriate to use of devout Christians, who have a robust ethical system and uphold a Bible-based standard of behavior. Christianity eschews idolatry, sexual immorality, murder, cruelty, theft, and myriads of other sins spoken against in the Bible. Many Christian denominations do not limit their definition of sin to the New Testament, either; for example, many forbid tattoos based on Leviticus 19:28.

The root of Christianity's blindness to the Torah is not antinomianism, or an antipathy toward laws and rules (though, as we will discuss in the next chapter, the extreme avoidance of "legalism" has sometimes resulted in overly permissive churches, a well-recognized problem within Christianity). In reality, the problem is totally different, and much deeper—it is tied with Christianity's understanding of God's covenants, specifically as they relate to the Jewish people—and how, by extension, Christianity fits into that covenant relationship. Christianity's blind spot is not really "law" as such; instead, it is God's continuing covenant relationship with Israel, Jews, and Judaism. The Torah is an inextricable part of that relationship.

Realizing this fact will keep the Messianic Gentile from a potential pitfall—the desire to take on language like "keeping the Sabbath," "a kosher diet," or similar terminology drawn from the world of Judaism. Take the laws of kashrut for example. It is tempting, once one has cleared his house of bacon-wrapped shrimp, to begin telling others that he is now eating "kosher." In reality, though, he has only taken one step toward obeying all of the Torah's dietary laws.[13]

To be able to call one's diet "kosher," one would not be able to eat at restaurants or on ceramic dishes prohibited by Torah because they have been in contact with unclean meat, or to eat packaged food without a hechsher (a kosher certification; many packaged foods contain pork-derived ingredients that are not obvious from the ingredient list on the label), or to eat any non-certified kosher meat (properly slaughtered, salted, sciatic nerve removed, etc.), or to be anything less than scrupulously and meticulously observant of the laws of chametz during Pesach, among other things.

Someone who has stopped eating unclean meat has certainly taken steps toward observance, and many of these steps are necessary and praiseworthy (according to Acts 15, three of the laws which the apostles specifically laid on non-Jewish believers were dietary);[14]

still, they have no platform to call themselves "kosher"—or, for that matter, to criticize anyone else for *not* keeping kosher.

The second reason that "antinomian" is an inappropriate epithet to ascribe to a Christian is simply that, in addition to being incorrect, it is offensive and rude. Learned Christians know what "antinomian" means; calling them antinomian is tantamount to claiming they have no moral code whatsoever.

There is no better way to turn someone off to your point of view than to insult them. Religious rhetoric gets particularly charged on Internet forums, blogs, and social networks. How often we forget that we are commanded to "love one another with brotherly affection [and] outdo one another in showing honor" (Romans 12:10)!

UNDESERVED CRITICISM: DOCTRINAL DIVISION

Many people who begin to take hold of their Jewish roots wonder why they were never taught this perspective in church. It is natural to begin wondering what else the church has gotten wrong. Particularly vulnerable are the Christological controversies of the fourth and fifth centuries, during which many important Christian doctrines were given authoritative formulations. Since the ecumenical councils at which these doctrines were formulated were so far removed from the early Jewish Christianity which characterized the apostolic faith, they are likely to be called into question.

Along with the adoption of a more Jewish way of looking at the Scriptures can also come a general deprecation of the Greek way of thinking, of Hellenism and of anything that is not overtly Hebrew or Jewish. And surely, as Orthodox Archimandrite Lev Gillet put it, "There is no reason why a purely Jewish expression of the Christian faith could not be as adequate or become as venerable as the Greek one."[15] In other words, as Christian doctrine has its roots in

Second Temple Judaism, there should be a way to articulate the core doctrines of Yeshua's identity in the Hebrew language, in a way that Second Temple Jews would have been able to understand.

There is nothing wrong with questioning what one has been taught. The Bereans were praised for doing the same (Acts 17:11). But it seems to me that people often have a difficult time modifying the belief system in which they grew up or in which they came to faith. Then, *when they do finally change, many tend to break with their mother faith entirely.* Their love for their former church is replaced not by the desire for reform or even by indifference, but by antagonism.

I have seen this pattern repeated over and over. A Christian will be turned on to the feasts and festivals or to the dietary laws, but instead of joyfully embracing the mitzvot, they grow resentful toward their communities, pastors, and fellow congregants. Instead of modifying their trajectory slightly to accommodate the new information they have received, they begin trying to change course entirely, and question everything. In a tragic display of confirmation bias, these well-meaning believers become open to any new information—right or wrong—that undermines their former way of life, while shutting out anyone who tries to keep them on course.

Fortunately, many Messianic Gentiles are showing a great deal of moderation and care in this regard. I know a number of Christian pastors who have seen the merit in Messianic theology and practice, and have embraced the feasts and even the dietary laws on some level, but have no desire to leave their denominations, or their particular theological and cultural distinctiveness, behind. One, an Independent Fundamental Baptist, restricts himself to clean meat and attends Erev Shabbat dinners, yet still puts on his suit and tie for church every Sunday morning and evening, and goes door-to-door every Saturday. Another, a Methodist, erected a sukkah in his backyard last year, yet proudly supports his denomination at the state and national level.

Many Christians have taken small steps like this, and still identify as Christians, practicing Christianity and adhering to Christian doctrine. They are also true Messianic Gentiles who affirm the role and calling of the Jewish people and the validity of the Torah. Though there is some tension in this identity, it is not a total contradiction, as much of Christian doctrine is based on an informed reading of the New Testament.

This is easy to verify by reading any systematic theology text-book for yourself. You will notice that theology is divided into several subdivisions; any theology of Israel or of the Jewish people is conspicuously absent. You will find bibliology, theology proper, Christology, pneumatology, eschatology, and ecclesiology—but never a concerted attempt to build a comprehensive theology of the Jewish people or the Torah.

Supersessionism in theology textbooks is assumed, not really argued. And yet it also is conspicuously absent in an overt sense from most of Christian theology. The attributes of God, the identity of Christ, the role of the Holy Spirit, the authority of the Scrip-tures—the development of these core doctrines was unfortunately influenced by supersessionism, but the core concepts behind them are Biblical. And while Christian doctrine would surely be improved by a realization of the role of the Torah and God's continuing cov-enant relationship with Israel, as well as a serious consideration of traditional Jewish interpretation and exegesis, it is dangerous and irresponsible to reject it totally.

RECOGNIZE THE GOOD

Even as they seek to reform their mother faith and bring a knowledge and awareness of Christianity's Jewish roots to those around them, Messianic Gentiles would do well to focus on what is good about Christianity. This is necessary for several reasons, not least of which is the fact that Messianic Gentiles, as stated above, *are Christians.* Just as important, though, is the impact this positive attitude will have on any effort to bring other Christians to recognize the Jewish roots of their faith.

Christianity has brought billions of people
to Yeshua, the Jewish Messiah and King
of the Jews. This is a non-trivial accomplishment.

It isn't difficult to find good things to say about Christianity. First, Christianity has brought billions of people to Yeshua, the Jewish Messiah and King of the Jews. This is a non-trivial accomplishment. Even some Jewish scholars have recognized the significance of this fact. In *Hilkhot Melakhim* 11:10–12, Maimonides credits Christianity with preparing the Gentile world for the arrival of King Messiah by spreading knowledge of the Bible far and wide.[16] If even those who do not claim Yeshua as Messiah can affirm the good that has come from Christianity, certainly believers should be able to as well.

Second, Christianity has helped uncountable numbers of poor, hungry, destitute, abandoned people. Myriads of counselees—drug abusers and alcoholics, victims of abuse, troubled spouses—have benefited from a pastor's biblical advice. From Carey and Wilberforce's campaigns against satī [17] in India to the modern phenomenon of "adopting" starving African children, Christians everywhere have expended their resources to help those less fortunate. Today, Christian orphanages in India take in abandoned children with nowhere else to turn, just as devout Christian George Müller did over a century ago in England.

Most of these people—the poor, the abandoned, the disenfranchised, and the abused—will never understand how Yeshua fulfilled the Passover. They may never taste matzah. They may never utter a single word of Hebrew or even be able to read the Bible in their own language. Yet they rely, just as we do, on the saving grace of God through Yeshua the Messiah.

The world we live in is so dysfunctional that the simple message of God's love, of a hope for future redemption, of faith in Yeshua, is all that many people will ever understand—or even need to hear— about God. Christianity's core message is today, just as it was in the apostles' day, a simple, biblical message for simple, hurting people.

The Christians who, throughout the ages, have propagated this message and tried to soothe the hurting, feed the hungry, and speak to social injustice have been *keeping the weighty matters of Torah*. Both Yeshua (Mark 12:31) and the Sages (Rabbi Hillel in b.*Shabbat* 31a and Rabbi Akiva in *Sifra, Kedoshim* 4:12) taught that love of neighbor is the essence of Torah. These are non-trivial accomplishments which speak to the robust, biblical ethical system which many devout Christians have embraced.

Third, Christianity has preserved the New Testament. Just as the Torah cannot truly be separated from the Jewish community and the Jewish interpretive tradition that has developed around it, so the New Testament cannot really be separated from the Christian community and Christian interpretive tradition. And just as Messianic Judaism takes issue with some Jewish interpretations of the Old Testament (especially as they concern the identity of the Messiah), so Messianic Gentiles are free to take issue with some Christian interpretations of the New Testament—especially as they concern the Torah and the Jewish people. But this does not require a separation from Christianity or a rejection of the whole body of Christian doctrine, a lot of which is well-founded on Scripture.

Fourth, Messianic Gentiles would not exist without Christianity. They have no direct relationship with the first-century church, the apostles, or the New Testament that has not already been mediated by Christianity—and this is not a bad thing.

One thing Messianic Gentiles must learn is that they do not have a direct, unmediated relationship with God. Jews have many covenants with God by virtue of their very existence as descendants of the Patriarchs. In contrast, Ephesians 2:12–13 describes the state of Gentiles as "separated from Christ, alienated from the commonwealth of Israel and strangers to the covenants of promise, having no hope and without God in the world. But now in Christ Jesus you who once were far off have been brought near by the blood of Christ." On this same theme, R. Kendall Soulen wrote:

> Israel's unique place in God's consummating plan means that it not only receives the gifts of creaturehood and childhood but also learns directly from God that this is so. This is the privilege that comes with Israel's identity as God's specially beloved child. In contrast, Gentiles receive the same benefits but [only] come to know about them through contact with the Jewish people.[18]

Gentiles only have a relationship with God as it has been mediated through the Jewish people, and through Messiah specifically. This concept is surprising to most Christians and is more thoroughly explored in the next chapter under the section "The Church and Israel." At this point, it must suffice to say that the Messiah is the Gentile's only bridge to God, and the concept of Messiah only exists as the fulfillment of prophecies and promises made to the Jewish people. Today, Gentiles can only know about Messiah through the text of the New Testament, which was collected and transmitted by the Christian church.

It is important for the Messianic Gentile not to lose sight of the work God has previously done in his life. He must never forget that the church has served an incredible purpose as the vehicle that brought him and billions of others to the knowledge of the God of Israel through preserving, propagating, and preaching the New Testament texts, and continues to serve as the visible body of Messiah to this day.

Pirkei Avot 6:3 contains a profound teaching that is particularly relevant here:

> Whoever learns from someone else a single chapter, a single law, a single verse, a single word, even a single letter, must treat him with honor, for so we find in the case of David, king of Israel, who learned only two things from Ahitophel, yet he called him his teacher, his guide, and his close friend, for so it says, "But it is you, my equal, my guide, my close friend" [Psalm 55:13]. The following inference can be derived: if David, king of Israel, who learned only two things from Ahitophel, called him his teacher, guide and close friend, how much more must one who learns from someone else

> a chapter, a verse, a word, or even a single letter, treat
> him with honor! And honor is due only to Torah, as
> it is written, "The wise shall inherit honor" [Proverbs
> 3:35], and "The wholehearted attain good," [Proverbs
> 28:10], and "good" signifies Torah, as it is said, "I have
> given you good instruction, do not forsake my Torah"
> [Proverbs 4:2].

Messianic Gentiles would do well to heed the teaching of this mishnah. Showing reverence towards one's teacher, even if what they learned was small—a single letter or verse—is showing reverence towards God and the Torah. Conversely, dishonoring one's teacher is in fact dishonoring God's work in one's life.

Messianic Gentiles have certainly learned from their Christian pastors and teachers. Cultivating a sincere gratefulness and reverence for the Christian teachers who have helped them along their spiritual walk will create and maintain an atmosphere of mutual respect, an atmosphere in which real dialogue can happen.

Another mishnah (*Pirkei Avot* 4:1) states,

> Ben Zoma said, "Who is wise? One who learns from
> everyone, as it is said, 'From all my teachers I have
> learned, for Your testimonies are my meditation'
> [Psalm 119:99]. Who is strong? One who masters his
> evil impulse, as it is said, 'He who is slow to anger is
> better than the mighty, and he who rules over his spirit
> is better than he who conquers a city' [Proverbs 16:32].
> Who is rich? One who rejoices in what he has, as it is
> said, 'When you eat from the labor of your hands, you
> will be happy and all will be well with you' [Psalm 128:2].
> 'You will be happy'—in this world, 'and all will be well
> with you'—in the World to Come. Who is honored? One

who honors others, as it is said, 'Those who honor Me, I will honor; but those that scorn Me will be despised' [1 Samuel 2:30]."

Our Master also spoke of honoring others instead of desiring a position of influence:

Now he told a parable to those who were invited, when he noticed how they chose the places of honor, saying to them, "When you are invited by someone to a wedding feast, do not sit down in a place of honor, lest someone more distinguished than you be invited by him, and he who invited you both will come and say to you, 'Give your place to this person,' and then you will begin with shame to take the lowest place. But when you are invited, go and sit in the lowest place, so that when your host comes he may say to you, 'Friend, move up higher.' Then you will be honored in the presence of all who sit at table with you. For everyone who exalts himself will be humbled, and he who humbles himself will be exalted." (Luke 14:7–11)

I frequently receive letters from people who are concerned that their adoption of the Messianic Gentile worldview will cause them to be ostracized in or excommunicated from their churches. In reality, the opposite can happen. Imagine being exalted and honored in the church. Imagine being told, "Friend, move up higher." This is exactly what Yeshua promised to those who humble themselves. If Messianic Gentiles cultivate this atmosphere of mutual respect, of honoring one another, by recognizing and affirming what is good in their mother faith, and by humbling themselves and remaining under the authority of pastors and church leaders, they can open the way for constructive dialogue and communication.

Lots of people have bad experiences in church. Perhaps they feel they are not learning enough, or they encounter people who struggle with the sins of hypocrisy and pride. It is tempting for the Messianic Gentile to find a solution in Judaism, a religion that appears from the outside to have no faults or problems. Yet there are numerous problems in Judaism, scandals and abuses that never reach non-Jewish ears due to the insular nature of the Jewish community. Every religion and belief system encompasses people who fail to live up to its ideals. Even the early church in Jerusalem, led by the apostles themselves, had problems, as recorded in the book of Acts—remember Aquila and Priscilla?

The Torah commands us to apply the same standard, to have just weights and fair measures in every situation (Leviticus 19:35–36; Proverbs 16:11). It is not fair to criticize Christianity based on the shortcomings of some of its adherents, and on the other hand, to overlook the shortcomings of observant Jews, and then use that evidence to claim that Judaism is legitimate while Christianity is not. In each religion there are shallow, prideful hypocrites; yet both Judaism and Christianity are based on the Scriptures and maintain a biblical standard of morality—whether their adherents always meet that standard or not.

I have made a personal commitment to reengage the church. With the exception of occasional opportunities that I had to speak in churches, I had not really been a part of the church for more than 25 years. As I saw the need for what I am proposing in this book, I made a commitment to a local Southern Baptist church here in my current place of residence. I was not sure what to expect. I was met with godly people, devout Christians who are dedicated to daily prayer, Bible study, and good deeds. I saw that many of my assumptions were wrong, and I realized that this is simply the way committed Christians live—they are devoted to the God of Israel.

They give tzedakah (charity); they help the less fortunate; they try very hard to live up to the Messianic ideal which Yeshua exemplified. Their heart for those that hurt is real; their desire to change the world for God is good; and they are as committed to learning and growing. But more than all of that, they are consistent in their service. Each time I leave town, the men in my Sunday school class offer to maintain my lawn; they check in on the well-being of my children; they keep me in their prayers while I am away.

Simple acts of service repair the world and establish Messiah's kingdom. One church in northern Ohio that uses our Torah Club material as the basis for their teaching programs actively supports their economically depressed community through an amazing food program. They essentially transformed their gymnasium into a mini-supermarket, and people from the community come in, choose their own food, push their own shopping carts, and are able to meet their families' needs in a dignified manner.

The Catholic Church has been the largest champion for the life of the unborn. On an international level, they have refused to allow the abortion of unborn children to become normative. Christians are the ones who have set up pregnancy crisis clinics around the globe as a means to support the mother and protect the child.

Myriads of Christians throughout history have distinguished themselves even more so, by heroic acts of goodness and kindness that exemplify the character of God. Take for example Dietrich Bonhoeffer, a German Lutheran pastor and theologian who died at the hands of the Nazis after spending his life trying to protect the Jewish people. His writings on Christian ethics and the imitation of

The Christian faith has inspired untold numbers
of ordinary human beings to do extraordinary
things for God and for other people.

Christ are still widely read today. Countless other Christians, like Corrie ten Boom and Irena Sendler, put their lives in danger on a daily basis in order to shelter and protect Jews from the Nazi regime.

Or consider Mother Teresa, who spent decades helping the poor and disenfranchised in India, inspiring an entire generation to consider the plight of those entrenched in poverty. Or Roger Williams, who for decades single-handedly kept the peace between the Native Americans and the Rhode Islanders, and whose insight laid the foundation for the modern concept of freedom of religion. Or Florence Nightingale, who was inspired by God to change the world of nursing, saving countless lives.

Many of these examples (and thousands more) are so famous as to be prosaic. Yet we must never forget that the Christian faith has inspired untold numbers of ordinary human beings to do extraordinary things for God and for other people.

At this point, there is one remaining objection. Someone will say that Christians are held to a higher standard than those of ages past. The argument goes something like this: God's spirit has revealed to us certain truths about the Jewishness of Yeshua and about the Torah that he did not reveal to Christians in past ages. Therefore, the great heroes of yesteryear were exempt from observing the mitzvot, while today's Christians are under judgment for their failure to observe them.

Yet this claim is disingenuous. God's spirit is indeed moving many to realize that Yeshua is Jewish, that the Torah is still relevant, that God's covenants with the Jewish people are still in force, and the kingdom of heaven is at hand. Yet this realization is still spreading. God did not reveal it to everyone at once. Those who have come to this realization are the ones responsible for showing it to others. If anyone is held to a higher standard, it is the Messianic Gentile, not the traditional Christian who has never been properly exposed to these ideas.

To put it simply, institutional Christianity has been an incredible vehicle for moving people toward Yeshua. While the institutional church has made unfortunate and terrible missteps, the people in it have brought untold good into the world. It is absolutely necessary to accept and internalize that truth before dealing with the problems in the church, because—as we all know—as great an institution as it is, the church needs to change.

> Any dispute that is for the sake of Heaven will have a constructive outcome; but one that is not for the sake of Heaven will not have a constructive outcome. What sort of dispute was for the sake of Heaven? The dispute between Hillel and Shammai. And which was not for the sake of Heaven? The dispute of Korach and his entire company. (*Pirkei Avot* 5:20)

May our dispute be for the sake of Heaven.

The Church Needs to Change

Seeds of anti-Judaism were unfortunately
planted in the church millennia ago.
Today, it blooms in full flower.

P eruse the shelf at your local Christian bookstore, and you might find some interesting titles:

◊ *Change Your Church for Good*

◊ *Why Nobody Learns Much of Anything at Church*

◊ *How to Change Your Church (Without Killing It)*

◊ *The Problem with Evangelical Theology*

This is just the tip of the iceberg. Dozens, maybe hundreds, of books have been written to help churches change their theology and praxis. Most, if not all, of these books are written from a fairly sympathetic perspective. They are not designed to undermine Christianity, but to strengthen it. These authors, and many others, recognize that there are problems that need to be fixed; some identify theological issues, others practical ones. Not all agree on the solutions, and not everyone even agrees on what the problems are—but all of these writers are agreed that change needs to happen.

The idea that the church needs to change is not new. The Protestant Reformation was based on the idea that the church needed to change; it was originally a movement of Catholics who sought to reform their own Catholic religion. Still today, the Lutheran liturgy is difficult for the uninitiated to distinguish from a Catholic Mass. Compared to modern Evangelical Christian worship services, the ancient liturgies appear to be quite similar. Yet Reformed Protestants retain their name today, a reminder of a time when they still protested what they perceived to be the problems in their mother church.

The church today is not without its reformers. Scot McKnight recently wrote a book called *The King Jesus Gospel*[19] in which he challenges the very heart of Evangelical preaching. McKnight and thousands of others have realized that the salvation message of modern Evangelical Protestantism is severely lacking, having been gutted of much of its power and removed from its biblical context. By reducing the entire gospel message to nothing more than "justification by faith," Evangelicals have missed so much of what it means to really follow Yeshua.

In critiquing the modern, reductionistic "gospel," McKnight addresses what I believe to be a key problem that plagues today's Christian church—the abandonment of the biblical gospel message for an oversimplified substitute. But this isn't the only issue I have with traditional Christian theology and practice.

During our ministry through First Fruits of Zion (a publishing ministry I founded over twenty years ago), we have identified four essential errors which have kept Christians from fully understanding the Scriptures, understanding their role and place in salvation history, and accomplishing the mission which God gave them. First, the Christian church has forgotten that Jesus was and is a practicing Jew. Second, Christians have forgotten the centrality of Israel in God's plan to redeem the world and her continued covenant status as God's chosen people. Third, Christianity has an extremely low view of the Torah itself and the commandments God gave to the Jewish people. Fourth, the Christian gospel message, having replaced the broad and majestic vision of the kingdom of heaven with a knowledge-based individualistic salvation, has been emptied of its power.

These four errors have corresponding truths. Jesus is Jewish; Israel is central; the Torah remains valid and applicable to Jewish and Gentile believers in differing ways; the kingdom of heaven is coming. Acceptance and application of these truths differentiate Messianic believers from mainstream Christians. This book is all about communicating these truths to Christians in a gentle, non-confrontational way.

But before we get to that, I want to remind you that Scot McKnight isn't alone. Many other Christian writers have begun to question, reinterpret, and redefine not only the functional aspects of Christianity—how the church functions and worships—but the theological underpinnings of Christianity. These concerns are not limited to seminaries and universities, either, but are coming out in popular books and videos. The shallowness and superficiality that have caused many Messianic Gentiles and others to become disenchanted with the church have driven many leading Christians to search for answers as well.

The former Bishop of Durham, N. T. Wright, a prolific and popular Christian author, has come under fire for his interpretation of the doctrine of justification, which he connects strongly to the concept of identity as a member of God's chosen people (sound familiar?).[20] Baptist preacher Paul Washer became an Internet sensation after telling thousands of young people at a large Christian conference that they were false converts because they had not seriously committed their lives to Yeshua; whether he was right or wrong, he caused millions of people to question the wisdom of pronouncing someone "saved" because they had said a quick prayer. Even megachurch pastor Joel Osteen has advocated observance of some of the Torah's dietary laws—in front of his entire congregation!

All of these authors and speakers have hit on important scriptural truths and attempted to make real, lasting theological changes in their churches and denominations. They have met with opposition and they have engendered controversy, but they have also experienced success. They have made a difference.

We can too.

YESHUA THE JEWISH MESSIAH

The most tragic mistake the church ever made was to forget that its Messiah is Jewish. I use the present tense purposefully; Yeshua is just as Jewish today as he was when he walked the hills of Galilee. Markus Bockmuehl relates the following:

> [New Testament scholars] who otherwise affirm the Jewish identity of Jesus are often content to sideline his resurrection as irrelevant. Even those who do take it seriously do not always make enough of one crucial fact: the one who is raised is none other than the crucified Messiah of Israel and "King of the Jews."[21]

In other words, the resurrected Yeshua is as much a Jew as is the miracle-working rabbi of the Gospels. Every day, millions of Christians pray to the God of Israel through their mediator, the King and Messiah of the Jews, Yeshua the Messiah. Yet they, for the most part, have remained blind to this fact. Dauermann's analysis is insightful and bears repeating:

> Examine the church's artistic and literary legacy and you will detect amnesia concerning the Jewishness of Yeshua. Instead, the church embraces a *generic Christ*, the *cosmic Savior*, the *Man for Others*, a *Metaphysical Hero*, a *Chameleon Redeemer* who blends in perfectly wherever he is found. In its paintings, icons, weavings, drawings, and sculptures, the church in every culture makes Jesus over in its own image. You will find the *Gentile Christ* with the aquiline nose, the rugged white *Anglo Saxon Marlboro Man Christ*, *African and Afro-American Christs*, *Asian Christs*, often in Buddhist

postures of meditative repose, *Indian Christs* looking more Guru than "Jewru," Swinburne's conquering
pale Galilean, Mexican Christos twisting in crucified
agony, and various *designer Christs*, tailored to fit each
consumer culture ... Jesus was, is, and evermore will
be a Jew. Healing this blind spot is crucial because the
Messiah of faith and the Yeshua of history only intersect
in this one who became incarnate in the very Jewish
womb of the Virgin Mary. Our faith in the Messiah is
groundless wherever we lose contact with his flesh and
blood specificity.[22]

Yeshua's admonishment of the Samaritan woman in John 4—
that she didn't know who she worshiped because she wasn't Jewish—
might find equal relevance directed at a modern Christian. Most
Christians don't know that they worship a Jewish rabbi from the
Second Temple Period. Most Christians don't know that the very
concept of a messiah is alien to any other context outside of Judaism.

The blind spot of Yeshua's Jewishness is the church's great
lacuna. More than any other single factor, this hole in Christian
theology is responsible for so many of Christianity's mistakes and
failures throughout history. As Yeshua is the Christian's only connection to the people and the scriptures of Israel, the church's
redefinition of Yeshua is the root of the other three serious problems
discussed below. Fortunately, as a result, addressing this one blind
spot opens the door for the complete restoration of the Christian
faith to its Jewish roots.

Yeshua's Jewishness is absolutely foundational for many reasons. First, it opens up the New Testament, which is a closed book
outside of the context of first-century Judaism. Interpreters have
offered thousands of different interpretations of New Testament

texts; without the understanding that Yeshua and his followers practiced Judaism, all of these interpretations appear to have merit. The world of biblical interpretation is therefore in a state of confusion and conflict.

An understanding of Yeshua's Jewishness and the Jewish context in which he lived has the potential to help resolve that conflict and illuminate the Gospels and Epistles so that their meaning can finally be understood. Rather than trying to draw from the text answers to questions that the text never sought to answer, an interpreter familiar with Jesus' Jewish context will be better able to discern what Yeshua was trying to communicate.

The parables of Yeshua provide a perfect example. Many Christian interpreters believe that Yeshua was cloaking secret, esoteric truths in seemingly simple stories, hiding his true message so that only his disciples would understand. This idea gives many interpreters the perceived freedom to offer their own teachings, claiming that they are the true, hidden, deeper meaning behind Yeshua's parables.

However, the parable in Judaism is used as a simplifying device, a way to communicate ideas clearly to people who may have difficulty understanding them.[23] Once one realizes that Yeshua taught as a Jewish teacher, he will begin looking for the plain meaning of Yeshua's message rather than seek for hidden truths. In this way, he will immediately begin to understand the teaching of the Master better.

Similarly, the recognition of Yeshua's Jewishness precludes certain interpretations of the Gospels. For example, Yeshua taught that the Temple was going to be destroyed. Based on one interpretation of Hebrews 8, many Christian interpreters assume that this tragic event was the result of the natural outworking of salvation history.

The Temple was old, outdated, and outmoded; Yeshua had come to bring something new.[24]

In a Jewish context, though, that interpretation holds no weight. Judaism, based on explicit prophecies throughout the Old Testament, looks forward to a Messianic Age in which the Temple continues to function. Yeshua's warning of the destruction of Jerusalem and of Herod's Temple was part of the same stream of prophetic revelation that caused Jeremiah to prophesy about the destruction of the first Temple (Jeremiah 7, esp. v.14). It was designed to provoke repentance, not to inaugurate a new religion or system of worship.

The understanding of Yeshua's Jewishness brings new life to his teachings and actions. And while one can derive some level of understanding from Yeshua's plain teachings—consider for example the impact of the Sermon on the Mount for Christian ethics—there is so much more to be apprehended, so much more that lies beyond the pale of traditional Christian interpretation.

The church needs to recognize Yeshua as a Jew. This single hurdle, if crossed, opens up a world of possibilities. If Yeshua was (and is) Jewish, then he practiced Judaism; many Christians who have realized this have developed respect for the entire corpus of Jewish literature. I know a local pastor who regularly consults the Midrash and other Jewish works when developing his sermons. Another has the entire Schottenstein Talmud Bavli displayed on his office shelf and is slowly going through each of its tractates—a significant investment of time and money.

If Yeshua was (and is) Jewish, then the Jews are his kindred people, and ever will be. This is discussed further below, yet it bears mentioning now that the entire gruesome history of the church's persecution of Jews could have been prevented with the realization of this simple fact. The church must see itself as part of a commonwealth working together with Israel, not as a replacement for Israel; this realization starts with the fact that her messiah, Yeshua, is a Jew and a proud member of the children of Israel.

If Yeshua was (and is) Jewish, then all of his arguments with the Pharisees were intra-Jewish disputes, in which certain foundational ideas—the relevance of Torah, the authority of the traditions of the elders, the framework of halachic formulation and debate, the election of the Jewish people—were taken for granted. This knowledge sheds great light on Yeshua's interaction with other Jews.

If Yeshua was (and is) Jewish, then he can more easily be understood as promoting and upholding the Torah and Jewish tradition in passages like Matthew 5:17–20 and 23:2–3. Based on his testimony in these passages, it can be assumed that he faithfully kept the covenant that God made with Israel on Mount Sinai. He wore tefillin and tzitzit; he was *shomer Shabbat* (observant of the Sabbath laws); he kept kosher.[25] Knowing this causes one to reassess the importance of the Torah, its continuing relevance, and its binding authority; on the other hand, without the context of Yeshua's Jewishness, the Torah remains a far-off and seemingly irrelevant concept to most Christians.

If Yeshua was (and is) Jewish, his teaching must be located on the map of greater Judaism. His prophetic rebuke should be seen in continuity with that of the earlier prophets. His core message, his "gospel," should not be seen as a call to abandon Judaism, but rather, it must be recognized as a call to covenant fidelity, a rallying cry to the Torah and its teachings.

All of these concepts find their roots in Yeshua's Jewishness. This, combined with the centrality of Yeshua in Christian thought and theology, makes understanding the Jewishness of Yeshua a vital first step for any Christian who wants to have any hope of moving forward toward a Messianic understanding of the Scriptures and of their own responsibilities and obligations to God.

Demonstrating Yeshua's Jewishness to a Christian audience is as simple as it is foundational, making this concept a great starting point for any conversation relevant to Messianic Gentile theology. Many authors have already made significant inroads toward a wide-scale recognition of Yeshua's Jewishness. On the popular level, Brad Young,[26] Lois Tverberg,[27] and my friends and colleagues at First Fruits of Zion,[28] among many others, have all endeavored to bring new life to Yeshua's words by returning them to their Jewish context. Multitudes of other works have been written at the scholarly level and continue to influence seminarians and doctoral candidates all over the world.

Introducing these concepts to mainstream Christians does not require a high level of learning, though Messianic Gentiles should endeavor to become basically literate in Judaism, and not just have a surface level understanding of their Jewish roots, before trying to communicate these concepts to others. Fortunately, the resources mentioned above can go a long way toward establishing some of this literacy.

The best avenue of approach when communicating Yeshua's Jewishness is simply to point out scriptural evidence that Yeshua was a practicing Jew. For example, Yeshua was born into an observant Jewish family, circumcised on the eighth day, and redeemed as the firstborn (the ceremony of *pidyon ha'ben*).[29] He went to synagogue every Sabbath.[30] He was reluctant to minister to Gentiles, and before his resurrection, he forbade his disciples to go to Gentile cities.[31] He was called "rabbi," a traditional term for a teacher of Judaism.[32] He celebrated the Jewish feasts of Passover,[33] Chanukah,[34] and Tabernacles.[35] It is not a great leap for Christians to consider the importance of these Jewish things when they realize that they did not play a trivial role in the life of their Messiah.

These concepts and many more are discussed in further detail in First Fruits of Zion's Torah Club Volume Four, as well as in dozens of other popular and scholarly books. Nevertheless, an incredible amount of work remains to be done in this area. Most Christians still have no idea that they are called to be disciples of a Jewish rabbi. The potential for Messianic Gentiles to come alongside these Christians and seriously impact their understanding of Yeshua's life and teachings is nearly limitless. "The harvest is plentiful, but the laborers are few" (Matthew 9:37).

THE CHURCH AND ISRAEL

Christianity began as a sect of Judaism. All but the most conservative scholars are now almost unanimously agreed on this fact. So what happened? How did the church forget its origins? How did the church go from a sect of Judaism to an intense persecutor of Judaism? Why does much of the church now define itself against Judaism, as the antithesis of Judaism?

Answering these questions has been a large part of the mission of First Fruits of Zion since its inception, as well as the Messianic Jewish restoration and the entire Torah movement. Understanding this ancient schism allows us to competently articulate why we continue to advocate the restoration of the Torah to its proper place and the rediscovery of Christianity's Jewish roots. It enables us to explain the origin of Christian supersessionism, anti-Semitism, and anti-Torah theology. It explains how the followers of Yeshua went from Judaism to anti-Judaism, and it explains why today they need to return to their Jewish roots.

Yet the answer to the question of Christian anti-Judaism is not simple. Scholars don't just argue over the details, either; the whole picture of how Judaism and Christianity came to be separated is extremely fuzzy. Some modern scholars question whether there was any "parting of the ways" before the rise of Islam. According to Paula Fredricksen, the *contra Judaeos* tradition of the church fathers—a series of pamphlets and sermons against the Jews and Judaism—belied the tendency of the average Christian to associate closely with the Jewish people. There would have been no need, she postulates, to discourage association with Jews if it were not a widespread phenomenon. So while many scholars place the separation of Judaism and Christianity in the second century or even earlier, Fredricksen sees evidence of a large degree of cooperation and peaceful coexistence at least into the sixth century.[36]

Yet it is clear that in the end, a certain theological viewpoint won out over whatever popular sentiments toward the Jewish people may have existed. The modern Christian theology of the Jewish people and their historical role and destiny is based on the writings of the Church Fathers, who in turn were selected and canonized based on their theological viewpoints. There is reason to believe that this self-reinforcing paradigm included an element of supersessionism from its very beginning in the first century; Mark Nanos believes that the epistle to the Romans (c. 55–58 CE) was written in part to head off a supersessionist tendency in the Roman churches.[37]

Anti-Jewish theology seems to have flowered in the second century; Justin Martyr's *Dialogue with Trypho* and Ignatius's epistles, both from this era, betray quite extreme anti-Jewish sentiments. Ignatius wrote in the tenth chapter of his epistle to the Magnesians, "It is absurd to profess Christ Jesus, and to Judaize." Justin related to Trypho that:

The circumcision according to the flesh, which is from Abraham, was given for a sign; that you may be separated from other nations, and from us; and that you alone may suffer that which you now justly suffer; and that your land may be desolate, and your cities burned with fire; and that strangers may eat your fruit in your presence, and not one of you may go up to Jerusalem. For you are not recognised among the rest of men by any other mark than your fleshly circumcision ... For we too would observe the fleshly circumcision, and the Sabbaths, and in short all the feasts, if we did not know for what reason they were enjoined you, namely, on account of your transgressions and the hardness of your hearts.[38]

Magnus Zetterholm theorized that Ignatius's community began to separate from the Yeshua-believing Jewish community in Antioch due to social pressures from the synagogue and from the Roman government after the First Jewish War.[39] Whatever the reason, though, it is clear that at some point, an entrenched, powerful segment of the established church leadership began to discourage Jewish practices, synagogue attendance, and maintaining a connection with the Jewish community. Yet it is evident that even in the fourth century, Asian Christians still calculated Easter (called *Paskha*) with reference to the Jewish Passover; the Council of Nicaea finally ruled that a different method was to be used in 325 CE.[40]

Whatever the situation may have been in the ancient world, though, the state of affairs in the modern, post-Crusades, post-Inquisition, post-Shoah (Holocaust) world is clear. Medieval Christianity made itself the Jewish people's worst enemy, and the church is still coming to terms with the theological ramifications of that fact. The study of Jewish-Christian relations has flourished since the Shoah, with dozens of volumes and at least one major journal dedicated to it; yet the breach is far from healed.

The core issue at hand is the answer to the question, "Who are the people of God?" To a traditional Christian, the answer is obvious—Christians are the people of God. For almost two thousand years, this mindset has left no room in Christian theology for any non-Christian to have any kind of meaningful relationship with God.

Conservative Christianity can almost be defined by its exclusivity. Jews are "out," Christians are "in." It has been this way since the days of Ignatius and Justin Martyr, who lived and taught during the formative years of the church.

Yet this viewpoint makes no sense of the Bible, or at least the eighty to ninety percent of the Bible that does not directly concern the Gentile mission of the New Testament church. The Bible deals with a very specific group of people from cover to cover; this group is called Israel and is defined as the nation which is descended from the man called Israel, Abraham's grandson, born as Ya'akov ben Yitzchak nearly four thousand years ago.

Consider the following Scriptures:

◊ Psalm 147:19–20: He declares his word to Jacob, his statutes and rules to Israel. He has not dealt thus with any other nation; they do not know his rules.

◊ 1 Chronicles 16:12–18: Remember the wondrous works that he has done, his miracles and the judgments he uttered, O offspring of Israel his servant, children of Jacob, his chosen ones! He is the Lord our God; his judgments are in all the earth. Remember his covenant forever, the word that he commanded, for a thousand generations, the covenant that he made with Abraham, his sworn promise to Isaac, which he confirmed to Jacob as a statute, to Israel as an everlasting covenant, saying, "To you I will give the land of Canaan, as your portion for an inheritance."

◊ Psalm 135:4: For the Lord has chosen Jacob for himself, Israel as his own possession.

◊ 2 Samuel 7:23–24: And who is like your people Israel, the one nation on earth whom God went to redeem to be his people, making himself a name and doing for them great and awesome things by driving out before your people, whom you redeemed for yourself from Egypt, a nation and its gods? And you established for yourself your people Israel to be your people forever. And you, O Lord, became their God.

I could fill pages and pages with similar verses. Throughout the Torah, the Prophets, the Writings, and the New Testament, Israel's unique role and calling is affirmed repeatedly, in plain language that anyone can understand. To remove Israel from her proper place as God's covenant people is to make the Bible incomprehensible.

Yet this is exactly what Christianity has, for the most part, done. Very few Christians enjoy reading through the books of the Kings or the Chronicles. Many Christians get lost when they try to read the Law or the Prophets. These books are so centered on the unique covenant people of Israel and her covenantal relationship with God that without this understanding, most of the Old Testament appears to be completely irrelevant.

But it's not irrelevant. Israel—the Jewish people—is still God's covenant people today. This is not to say that Gentiles have no place in God's plan or that they cannot be God's people or that God's covenants are irrelevant to Gentiles. On the contrary, the apostles were adamant that Gentiles could be included as God's people without becoming Jewish.

What I am saying, though, is that the center, the focus of God's activity in the world, is the people of Israel. As Paul wrote (Romans 9:4–5): "They are Israelites, and to them belong the adoption, the glory, the covenants, the giving of the law, the worship, and the promises. To them belong the patriarchs, and from their race, according to the flesh, is the Christ, who is God over all, blessed forever. Amen."

Most Christians and even many Messianic Gentiles have failed to recognize the absolute centrality of Israel, the Jewish people, in God's plan and purpose. This is usually not through any moral or intellectual fault of their own, nor is it usually out of any kind of antipathy toward the Jewish people; rather, most people have no reason to question a venerable, two-thousand-year-old theological matrix. After all, it's not as if Christians haven't tried to read the Bible. It's just that they don't always have the context to be able to appreciate Israel's identity, role, and calling in God's plan. So when confronted with passages which repeatedly affirm this identity, Christian theologians have come up with a multitude of explanations. Most Christians today have a theology of Israel that is drawn from one of two sources: Reformed theology or Dispensationalism.

Classical Reformed theology, as embraced by popular modern-day theologians, has absolutely no place for the Jewish people except as the recipients of a cursed "covenant of works." The election of Israel as an ethnic body, the physical sons of the man Israel, is completely ignored; it is a non-issue as far as eternal salvation is concerned. True "Israel" in Reformed theology has always been the church, the "elect," those who have faith; the Jewish people have been deemed as essentially irrelevant. Generally, people who embrace this theology tend to be anti-Zionist; Gary Burge is an outstanding example and has written several anti-Zionist books and speaks at anti-Zionist seminars.

Dispensationalism has proven to be immensely popular over the past century; its adherents have developed a reputation for being supporters of Israel and the Jewish people.

Dispensationalism, a popular movement of the late nineteenth- and twentieth-centuries, has advocated a different view. Dispensationalists believe that at least some of God's covenants with Israel—particularly the land-covenant—are still in force. Dispensationalists predicted the 1948 restoration of Israel to the Jewish people; that event was perceived as a substantial vindication of their theology. Dispensationalists therefore tend to be Christian Zionists.

Dispensationalism has proven to be immensely popular over the past century; its adherents have developed a reputation for being supporters of Israel and the Jewish people. While there are some serious deficiencies in the Dispensationalist paradigm (such as the low view of the Torah it shares with the rest of Christianity), the realization of the continuing relevance of Israel and the Jewish people is a great touchstone for starting and continuing dialogue about Yeshua's Jewishness and the role of the Torah in shaping God's relationship with the Jewish people and with Gentile believers.

Yet Reformed theology, along with its Calvinist worldview and anti-Zionist stance, has been growing in popularity. Traditional Reformed churches—Lutheran, Presbyterian, Episcopal—will be less open—even hostile—to a Christian Zionist or Dispensational viewpoint. At the same time, though, Reformed scholarship is opening the door to a more biblical, more "Jewish" perspective on the New Testament. Krister Stendahl, who in 1960 penned the remarkably prescient essay "The Apostle Paul and the Introspective Conscience of the West,"[41] was a Lutheran, a member of the Church of Sweden. Augsburg Fortress, a Lutheran publishing house, puts out some of the leading materials on the "Radical New Perspective on Paul," a movement whose theology substantially vindicates the Messianic perspective.

Catholics have made their own strides toward recognizing God's continuing relationship with the Jewish people. The landmark papal declaration *Nostra Aetate* radically decried the historic persecution of the Jewish people by the Church and repudiated anti-Semitic beliefs that the church had historically propagated. This makes the Catholic Church's view of the Jewish people the most progressive of any Christian denomination; they were the first to begin to repudiate anti-Jewish theology from the top down.

These victories are relatively small, and the average Catholic or Reformed Christian still does not understand the continuing role of the Jewish people as God's covenant nation. Yet the pastors, priests, and bishops in these denominations have been exposed to these ideas in the academic world and awareness continues to grow. If history is any guide, post-supersessionist scholarship will eventually percolate down to local priests and pastors and begin to influence churchgoers of all denominations.

The role of the Messianic Gentile in this process is vital. The well-grounded Messianic Gentile, who understands the historic and continuing role of the Jewish people as God's covenant nation, can be a noble presence in Christian churches, contributing a gracious and patient perspective toward Jews who have not yet embraced Yeshua as Messiah. Even one voice to head off the anti-Jewish rhetoric that often finds its way into teachings, sermons, and church curriculums can make a difference and cause people to question their assumptions.

True, it is challenging to be the single voice against a consensus of triumphalism and supersessionism. But when that voice comes from an entrenched, dedicated, devout member of the congregation, and when it speaks knowledgeably and deliberately, full of love, grace, and patience, it can and will make a difference.

When the church recognizes its connection with Israel, great things will happen. When Christians give to Jewish charities, it helps, though ever so slightly, to undo centuries of ill treatment and persecution. When Christians support Israel in the midst of the ever-present threat of militant terrorist organizations, it is a powerful statement that is not lost on the Jewish people.

Furthermore, when Christians recognize Israel's place and plan, they are in a position to fulfill the commandment that the apostles themselves laid on them: to remember the poor in Jerusalem and to support the Jewish people in time of need; Paul saw this as an absolute necessity, as Gentile Christians have benefited so greatly from the Jewish spiritual heritage (Romans 11:27; Galatians 2:10).

Finally, when Christians recognize the irrevocable calling and destiny of Israel, they are in a place to develop a more biblical ecclesiology and self-understanding. Instead of usurping Israel's identity and calling, Gentile Christians who understand Israel's identity can form a concrete identity of their own, one that is biblically based and complementary to that of the Jewish people, one that expands into the entire eschatological view of the Prophets of Israel.

For example, consider the beauty of Isaiah 56:6–7:

> And the foreigners who join themselves to the Lord, to minister to him, to love the name of the Lord, and to be his servants, everyone who keeps the Sabbath and does not profane it, and holds fast my covenant—these I will bring to my holy mountain, and make them joyful in my house of prayer; their burnt offerings and their sacrifices will be accepted on my altar; for my house shall be called a house of prayer for all peoples.

Toby Janicki wrote at length about this passage; to sum up his analysis, the Gentiles who join themselves to Israel must remain Gentiles in order for the passage to make sense. If they were proselytes, the Temple would not really be a "house of prayer for all peoples," as proselytes are accounted as Jews.[42]

Consider how powerful an opportunity is available for traditional Christians to realize their relationship to the Jewish people and how it helps to define their own role in God's consummative plan—if Messianic Gentiles would only graciously bring them nearer to this understanding.

THE CHRISTIAN AND THE TORAH

The third major historical error of mainstream Christianity is its failure to recognize the Torah as a permanent, binding authority over the Jewish people, and an expression of the heart of God as to his unalterable will for his covenant people.

While we discussed above that "antinomian" is an inappropriate moniker for Christians, it is true that Christianity has an unfortunately low view of the Torah. A few misunderstood passages in Paul's letters along with a few misinterpretations of Yeshua's teachings have effectively canceled most of the Old Testament. The ubiquitous Gideon New Testaments, which include only Psalms and Proverbs from the Old Testament, are a testament to how underappreciated and underutilized the Hebrew Scriptures are in the Christian church. Seminaries tend to encourage a higher level of proficiency in Greek than in Hebrew, indicating that the same attitude exists in the scholarly world.

Along with the diminished role of the Torah and the Old Testament, many Christian denominations eschew "works" in general. One popular Bible memory verse website lists Ephesians 2:8 as among its top ten verses, with 2:9 not far behind: "For by grace you have been saved through faith. And this is not your own doing; it is the gift of God, not a result of works, so that no one may boast." It seems that if there is one thing Christians know about good works, it's that they don't get you into heaven.

This attitude is even more prevalent in mainstream Evangelical Christianity. While Catholics and more traditional Reformed denominations have long traditions of high moral standards and long lists of rules, Evangelical Protestantism, as discussed further below, has cultivated a "salvation culture" in which the decision a person makes to accept Yeshua is the defining aspect of the Christian life.[43] Anything outside that decision is often thought to be relatively unimportant and of little lasting consequence—except, of course, for the vital task of evangelism (convincing others to make that same decision).

The Torah, on the other hand, takes for granted the initial decision of the individual, as a member of God's people, to accept the sovereignty of God. It is primarily concerned with what happens after that and what the life of God's people is supposed to look like. The restoration of this aspect of Christian living to the Evangelical church would be an incredible boon to the Christian faith.

Messianic Gentiles are not alone in their concern with post-salvation living. Many Christian authors, like Dallas Willard and Richard Foster, have popularized the importance of Christian disciplines, serious commitment, and righteous living. But the underlying doctrinal presupposition—that once someone is saved, their destiny is secure and consequently their actions don't really matter—still has a chokehold on Evangelical theology.

The devastating ramifications of this theology for the church are immediately apparent. The church's divorce rates are incredibly high. Modesty in many churches is almost non-existent. Large numbers of churches find it impossible to keep young people engaged in a lifestyle that proclaims to be holy yet does not really differentiate itself from the world surrounding it.

The good news is, the flagrant casting aside of God's standards by many modern Evangelical Christian churches is an aberration in church history. Only a few hundred years ago, John Wesley recorded in his journals how he got into serious trouble with his community for refusing communion to a member of his congregation who had sinned and not yet repented. Early church writings such as 1 Clement and the Didache also emphasize the paramount importance of obedience and holiness.

There are really two reasons for the modern abandonment of these concepts by many churches. The root problem is the church's failure to recognize its role and calling to repair the world along

> The best way to uphold the beauty, rightness, and
> goodness of a Torah-centered life is simply to live
> it. This would go farther than any argument, no
> matter how well thought out or biblically based.

with Israel through obedience to the commandments of God. Reestablishing the church's connection with Israel will go a long way toward enabling her to recognize her responsibilities and how they are informed by God's Torah.

The second reason for the modern church's permissiveness—at least that of the Protestant church—lies at the very heart of its gospel message. By reducing the gospel to nothing more than justification by faith, Christianity has unwittingly divested the gospel of its power. This is a problem all its own and will be explored below.

The best way to counter this theology is not, as I can testify by experience, to debate against it. I tried for many years to argue with the church as to the importance of good works, *tikkun olam* (repair of the world), and the beauty of the Torah, only to be rejected as "legalistic." This approach engenders controversy and bitter recriminations more often than not.

I and thousands of others have found that the best way to uphold the beauty, rightness, and goodness of a Torah-centered life is simply to live it. If all Messianic Gentiles lived blameless lives, so that no one could realistically expect to say anything negative about them and be believed (1 Peter 2:12, 3:16), this would go farther than any argument, no matter how well thought out or biblically based. The Torah is designed so that people who live out its ideals conspicuously resemble the Torah's author, God himself, and draw attention to him (Deuteronomy 4:5–8).

And while these laws were originally given only to Israel, Messianic Gentiles have been given significant obligations as well. The apostles used the Torah as a framework to inform the obligations of the Messianic Gentile; most of the Torah's 613 commandments are relevant to believing Gentiles in some way.[44] In fact, the apostles never anticipated the Gentile members of the *ecclesia*[45] becoming a church so distant from its foundational origins; they undoubtedly would have made these obligations clearer had they seen how radically the church was to break with Judaism. Much of what we are trying to do in our restoration of the Tent of David is repair these kinds of fundamental flaws that have developed in the theology of today's church.

At any rate, Messianic Gentiles should certainly be prepared to graciously and respectfully defend their way of life from the Scriptures (1 Peter 3:15). But the path that leads to respect for God's commandments does not begin with debate, but with teaching by example, with righteous living, with the active pursuit of *tikkun olam*.

I am convinced that if the message of submission to the authority of Yeshua the Messiah and to the obligations the apostles laid on his Gentile followers is presented correctly, the church is more than ready to accept it. Christians are hungry for a deeper, more meaningful spiritual experience; the Torah's richness and depth are more than sufficient to satisfy that hunger. The New Testament teaches clearly that Yeshua is equated with the Word, the *logos*, God's wisdom as recorded in the Old Testament. Presented in this light, the Torah is an attractive, beautiful, biblical solution to many of the ills suffered by churches struggling with shallowness and superficiality.

THE GOSPEL OF THE KINGDOM OF HEAVEN

The center of the Christian message is called the "gospel." The word comes from "God-spell" and literally means "good news." The Greek word which lies behind "gospel" in the New Testament is *evangelion*, which also means "good news." But what is this good news? What is the gospel message?

Modern Evangelical Christianity, which takes its name from the Greek word above, has a very strong, almost monolithic answer to this question. The gospel is that Yeshua the Messiah died for our sins, and that we can have eternal life by mentally or intellectually acknowledging that Yeshua is the Messiah and Son of God, and "accepting" Yeshua into our hearts.

This is the gospel that all Evangelical mission organizations try to get people to accept. From Bill Bright's famous "Campus Crusade for Christ" to Ray Comfort's "Way of the Master" and everything in between, though they all may disagree on everything else, their presentation of the gospel is exactly the same. Accept Jesus as Son of God and Savior; go to heaven when you die. Reject Jesus (or be unfortunate enough not to hear about him); go to hell.

Good news, right?

Here is what Regent College professor John Stackhouse says about this "gospel message":

> Over and over, students have betrayed an understanding of salvation that amounted to a sort of spiritual individualism that is little better than Gnosticism. In fact, we could make an important start simply by teaching that salvation is not about "Christians going to heaven." Salvation is about God redeeming the whole earth ... Salvation is about heading for the New

Jerusalem, not heaven: a garden city on earth, not the
very abode of God and certainly not a bunch of pink
clouds in the sky ... And salvation is not only about
what is to come but also about what is ours to enjoy
and foster here and now.[46]

Consider the vast implications of the preceding statement.
Instead of Yeshua being "the way, the truth, and the life" (John

When dogma is elevated above the very core of
Yeshua's message, above the message of the apostles,
of the prophets, and of the Torah, then it ceases to
be useful and instead becomes a barrier that keeps
people from engaging the Scripture objectively.

14:6), Christians have been taught that the acceptance of a certain
theological paradigm or definition of Jesus allows one to become
one of God's people. Instead of a world-changing message that has
the power to bring the kingdom of heaven into reality, the Christian
gospel has become a message about "me," about individuals and how
they can find eternal happiness.

While many leading Christian voices, from Paris Reidhead to
Scot McKnight, have spoken out against this watering down of the
gospel to nothing more than the acceptance of facts, the popular
misconception of Evangelical Christianity is still that believing
certain facts gets one "saved," and that this is the pinnacle of spiritual experience.

A key word in Stackhouse's assessment of Evangelicalism is the term "Gnosticism." Gnostics taught a lot of things, but their basic philosophy of salvation was that one was saved by having the right knowledge. So while early Christianity repudiated Gnosticism along with its entire doctrinal system, a premise that sounds suspiciously Gnostic—that knowing the right things will lead to salvation—has found its way directly into the heart of the Christian message.

To be fair, Gnostics and Christians would totally disagree on what this saving knowledge actually is, and even on the nature of that knowledge. Gnostics sought out esoteric knowledge that could not be known from empirical evidence, while Christians maintain that their gospel is plainly stated in the Scriptures. But evangelical Christianity's emphasis on having the right formulation of doctrine, the right Christological and soteriological knowledge, the role of assent to that specific knowledge as the mechanism by which one attains salvation, and the fact that this knowledge had to be supernaturally revealed in each system leads one to question whether Christianity was able to fully excise the Gnostic gospel.[47]

It is important that, as we seek to re-implement Yeshua's original plan and message, that we reassess the role of dogma—the idea that we must believe certain things that cannot be proven or supported directly from Scripture—in our faith. Christianity has traditionally taught that one must assent to a certain theological paradigm to be saved, regardless of repentance and faith. In fact, the very words "repentance" and "faith" are twisted in many Christian circles to mean nothing more than assent to dogma. A colleague of mine who went to a Baptist college assures me that the teachers there uniformly defined "repentance" as "belief in Jesus."

I am not saying that theology is not important, or that bad theology is not harmful; it is. However, when dogma is elevated

Yeshua surely preached the gospel; his
message—"Repent, for the kingdom of heaven
is at hand"—is just as much "the gospel"
today as it was two thousand years ago.

above the very core of Yeshua's message, above the message of the apostles, of the prophets, and of the Torah, then it ceases to be useful and instead becomes a barrier that keeps people from engaging the Scriptures objectively. The centrality of dogma has kept many intelligent, thinking people from having their questions about Yeshua and God answered honestly. Christianity's tenacious insistence and reliance on dogma will continue to weaken the entire belief system as far as it removes Christians from an authentic, biblically-based life of faith.

Scot McKnight has recently and comprehensively assessed the watering down of the modern gospel in a book called *The King Jesus Gospel*. McKnight's book is one of the most important books to hit Christian bookstore shelves in years. In it, he questions the idea that the entire good news of Yeshua can be reduced to "justification by faith." Is Yeshua dying for our sins really the entire gospel message?

If so, why wasn't Yeshua's public message something like "Believe that I will die for your sins, and you will inherit eternal life?"

McKnight recalls the views of several Christian pastors on the subject of the gospel as it is presented in the Gospels. One internationally known pastor searched the entire Gospel corpus to find the Pauline doctrine of justification by faith; he located something like it in Luke 18 (the parable of the tax collector and the Pharisee). He concluded that yes, Yeshua preached Paul's gospel. But McKnight asks—shouldn't it be the other way around? Shouldn't we defer to Yeshua and the twelve apostles and then see if Paul preached *their* gospel?

He records another chilling encounter he had with a pastor while he was writing his book. This pastor believed that Jesus didn't preach the gospel at all. He didn't know about it; no one understood the Christian gospel until the apostle Paul.[48]

Yeshua surely preached the gospel; his message—"Repent, for the kingdom of heaven is at hand"—is just as much "the gospel" today as it was two thousand years ago. When Peter adjured the crowds after the coming of the Spirit on Shavuot in Acts 2:38–39, his message was not "believe in Jesus; go to heaven." It was "Repent and be baptized every one of you in the name of Jesus Christ for the forgiveness of your sins, and you will receive the gift of the Holy Spirit. For the promise is for you and for your children and for all who are far off, everyone whom the Lord our God calls to himself."

Notice several things about this exhortation. First, repentance, not baptism, is primary. Second, "the promise" of the giving of the Holy Spirit is specifically given to a corporate people, Israel: "for you"—that is, those Jews and proselytes who were present—"and for your children"—that is, the next generation of Jews—"and for all who are far off"—those Jews in the Diaspora who had not made the pilgrimage to Jerusalem that year. (The Gentile mission did not enter Peter's mind until eight chapters later, in Acts 10.)

Finally, notice that Peter does not mention any kind of eternal reward. The incentive to repent and be baptized is not heavenly bliss. The Bible does, of course, speak of eternal life, but not here. In Peter's mind, as he gives the gospel of the kingdom to thousands of Jews, the impetus to receive the gospel is in order to be able to receive the spirit of God, which in turn empowers people to change the world

here and now, making the kingdom of heaven manifest and bring-
ing the presence and reign of God into the world in a tangible way.
Peter must have had in mind Matthew 28:18–20, the famous
"Great Commission" of Yeshua to his disciples, which also has a

Replacing the modern reductionist gospel with
the gospel of the kingdom is one of the most
difficult and yet one of the most potentially
fruitful reformations a Christian can make.

markedly different focus than today's popular gospel message: "And
Jesus came and said to them, 'All authority in heaven and on earth
has been given to me. Go therefore and make disciples of all nations,
baptizing them in the name of the Father and of the Son and of the
Holy Spirit, teaching them to observe all that I have commanded
you. And behold, I am with you always, to the end of the age.'"

Notice again the complete absence of believing that Yeshua
died for one's sins, or of any mention of eternal life. The gospel is
here and now; it requires a change in action in response to a call to
repentance. Yeshua's disciples were not called to make nothing more
than intellectual converts (though the gospel message does *include*
intellectual assent to certain statements), but to make disciples,
teaching them to obey Yeshua's commandments. This is how Yeshua
desired the kingdom of heaven to be expanded.

This idea—the kingdom of heaven—is at the center of Yeshua's
message. The term refers to the Messianic Age, when the Messiah
rules over Israel in a state of blessing and peace, regathers the exiles,

and implements justice and righteousness. At the core of Yeshua's message is the idea that in some way, this kingdom can be brought into existence now, through the actions of those who take on themselves the yoke of the kingdom.[49]

That is the gospel message. Repent—change the way you live your life and begin to obey the commandments of God. For the kingdom of heaven is at hand—you can, in some way, bring God's rule down to earth through your actions; it is possible to "live now for the realization of this Messianic Age."[50]

Replacing the modern reductionist gospel with the gospel of the kingdom is one of the most difficult and yet one of the most potentially fruitful reformations a Christian can make. Because the gospel is so central to Christianity and because Evangelical Christians have reduced it to such a short formula, anything bigger or grander in scope might be seen as heresy, as "adding to the gospel."

At the same time, though, precisely because the gospel is so central to Christianity, the potential for reform in this area is huge. Because Christians rely so heavily on the gospel, they will want to know as much about it as they can. If they have gotten something wrong in this area, they want to know. A positive approach to the Christian gospel is vital, yet the Messianic Gentile must be ready to expand the knowledge of the church in this area. Affirm what is good about the Christian gospel, and bring out its fullness.

Introducing the gospel of the kingdom requires the Messianic Gentile to be familiar with the relevant texts. He must know Yeshua's message well, so that he can prove easily from the gospels that Yeshua did not simply teach "believe in me and go to heaven when you die." He must also be able to articulate how Paul's message was also more nuanced and complex than simply "justification by faith," and how Paul's doctrine of justification was specifically oriented toward the inclusion of Gentile believers, as argued by scholars like Krister Stendahl and James Dunn; D. Thomas Lancaster's *The Holy Epistle to the Galatians* is particularly helpful here as well.

A HIGH CALLING

These four pillars—Yeshua the Jewish Messiah, the irrevocable calling of the Jewish people, the continuing relevance of the Torah, and the all-encompassing gospel of the kingdom of heaven—are the unique hallmarks of a concrete, biblical, Messianic Gentile worldview. The mission of the Messianic Gentile is to bear witness to these foundational concepts.

The task of communicating these four concepts to the institutional church may seem monumental. Each time the church forgot one of these core ideas, it adopted a corresponding error—the non-Jewish Jesus, supersessionism, the low view of Torah, and the watered-down gospel of intellectual assent. Some of these errors have been an integral part of Christian theology and self-identity for almost two thousand years. They are embraced by hundreds of denominations and organizational structures representing hundreds of millions of people.

It is true that the task to change the church is difficult. It represents one of the greatest challenges the Messianic movement will ever have to overcome. Yet it is prophetically necessary, it is vital, and the effort is absolutely worthwhile. It is truly a high and noble calling to engage the church and address these concepts. I hope that reading this chapter has helped you understand these foundational ideas so that you have the knowledge to be able to address them in a Christian context.

But that's not enough. Being informed, being studied, and understanding the problem and its solution are not enough. Restoring the

Tent of David requires that the servants of Messiah prepare themselves to be the kind of people God can use to deliver this message to the world and to Christian churches. In the next chapter, we will explore how to become that kind of person.

As we continue, though, take heart; the mission does not depend solely on us. We must all remember the role of God's spirit, who moves to help people understand, and to help people communicate these concepts. The Messianic movement was not born of the will of men; it has always been a move of God's spirit to draw his people closer to him, and to restore what has been lost. While we must be diligent and equip ourselves for the mission, in the end, our success depends on God. The most important thing we can do is bathe this mission in prayer and petition the Father for help, strength, and success.

Becoming a Shaliach

The path to successful change begins
with changing ourselves.

t should be clear by now that in order to accomplish the mission the Father has for many Messianic Gentiles, more preparation is required than simply being able to debate theological issues. Going to church and starting arguments, or trying to surreptitiously undermine the church's leadership, are recipes for failure and disaster. I have seen heavy-handed tactics fail completely, *even when the effort to introduce these concepts is led by the senior pastor!*

To reintroduce Christians to their Jewish Messiah, one must become a *shaliach*—a sent one, an ambassador, a missionary. The *shaliach* (plural: *shlichim*) in ancient times was a messenger who took on the status of representing his master, to the extent that he was accepted and treated as if he were actually the physical presence of the one who sent him. The Mishnah relates that a person's *shaliach* is like himself.[51]

To be a *shaliach* for the Messiah, then, we must be like him. Paul alluded to this fact when he wrote to the Colossians (3:10) that they had "put on the new self, which is being renewed in knowledge after the image of its creator." To bear the image of the Creator is to resemble Yeshua. It is to reflect God's loving kindness into the world. This concept—imitation of our Master—is at the heart of introducing people to the Jewishness of Yeshua.

True imitation of our Master was practiced by no one better than Paul, who left Jerusalem, the Temple, and the apostolic community behind to go through the Diaspora and spread the message of the kingdom. Despite being highly educated and Torah observant, he spent years overseas, where keeping the Torah is much more difficult, for the sake of the Master's call.

It is possible, in an attempt to apply this concept of imitation, to meet with disastrous results. For instance, one might feel called to issue a prophetic rebuke to the Christian church, in the vein of

Yeshua's polemic against the Pharisees (Matthew 23:13–39). For such a person, to imitate Christ would mean to condemn Christianity, to publicly call out Christians for their faults and failings.

This is a serious error. Yeshua's public, prophetic imprecations were only a small part of his ministry, and derived from his formal office as a prophet (the "prophet like Moses" of Deuteronomy 18:15–19). Not all believers are prophets, entitled to speak as if they were the voice of God, calling down judgment and condemning and correcting others. To take on this responsibility without being called to it is an extremely serious sin (Jeremiah 23:21).

Rather, Yeshua's teaching to his own disciples was to "first take the log out of your own eye, and then you will see clearly to take the speck out of your brother's eye" (Matthew 7:5). Yeshua is, in all probability, using sarcasm here. Once we have examined ourselves and begun the task of removing the leaven of hypocrisy from our own lives, we "see clearly" how futile and petty it is to try to correct everyone around us.

Far from pronouncing judgment and condemnation and trying to constantly correct others, Yeshua taught his disciples to be peacemakers, merciful, meek, humble, patient, and longsuffering, even under persecution (Matthew 5:1–10). Rather than boasting about *being* right, we should seek to *do* what is right.

A similar teaching is found in *Pirkei Avot* 1:12: "Hillel said: 'Be among the disciples of Aaron, loving peace and pursuing peace, loving people and drawing them close to Torah.'" Yeshua's affinity with Hillel is clear here. The Lord's brother, James the Just, also taught that an attitude of peaceful conciliation produces fruit, in his epistle (3:17–18): "But the wisdom from above is first pure, then peaceable, gentle, open to reason, full of mercy and good fruits, impartial and sincere. And a harvest of righteousness is sown in peace by those who make peace."

Other apostles and leaders in the early church had uniformly the same message. Paul wrote (Romans 12:18), "If possible, so far as it depends on you, live peaceably with all." The author of Hebrews wrote (12:14), "Strive for peace with everyone, and for the holiness without which no one will see the Lord."

Messianic Gentiles must not engage the topic of Yeshua's Jewishness from a negative, aggressive standpoint. It bears no fruit. It draws no one to the Torah. Peace, honor, and love are the only way forward.

PITFALLS ON THE ROAD TO RESTORATION

There are several pitfalls into which it is possible to fall on the road to restoring Yeshua's Jewishness to the Christian faith. One particularly serious pitfall is the temptation to look, dress, and act like orthodox Jews (for example, wearing *kippot* and conspicuously donning tzitzit), and/or claiming to be Jewish.[52]

One might think that this course of action would "provoke the Jews to jealousy" (Romans 11:14). Perhaps if Jews see Gentiles living as Jews, presumably doing a better job of it than the Jewish people, the Jews will become jealous, and somehow be drawn to Yeshua or to the Messianic movement.

However, this method of approach will consistently fail. Jews will be provoked, yes—but to anger and confusion, not to jealousy. Jews understand that the heritage of Judaism and of the Torah and of Jewish cultural distinctiveness is the unique possession of the Jewish people. Moreover, highly observant orthodox Jews represent a modest percentage of the Jewish people; consequently, seeing non-Jews without a supporting context attempting to emulate orthodox Jews, or pretending to live or represent this standard, is counterproductive.

Seeing Gentiles usurp this identity and heritage without respect to the unique covenant status of the Jewish people would be enough to anger even many secular Jews who are not invested in Judaism.

Traditional Christians, for the most part, also understand that there is something very wrong with pretending to be religious Jews. The Jewish cultural lifestyle carries no particular attraction to a grounded, spiritually healthy non-Jewish Christian. Seeing non-Jewish believers act like religious Jews is confusing and is likely to result in the offending group or person being marginalized and rejected. This behavior has the potential to isolate Messianic Gentiles from their culture, their communities, and sadly, even their families.

This is not to imply that Messianic Gentiles should not seek to implement the commandments of Torah to which they are actually obligated. But if a Messianic Gentile decides to go further than obeying the commandments, and begins wearing *kippot* regularly (a distinctly Jewish tradition not commanded in the written Torah), conspicuously wearing tzitzit (they are much less of an obstacle to others when they are tucked in), constantly wearing hats (even in church where it is often considered offensive), growing long beards and *payot*, and taking on other aspects of religious Jewish identity, he is in danger of causing unnecessary confusion and conflict.

The scope of this book does not explore in detail the problems that the misuse of these identifiers causes both for the Christian but also for the Jewish people. When these religious and cultural identifiers are applied by non-Jews, it is a huge problem and works against this mission. Christians need to have a clear sense of self-identity and a love for the Torah without disrespecting Jewish people. Messianic Gentiles can fulfill all of their obligations to the Torah without taking on distinctly Jewish practices. They are not called to become Jews, as the New Testament makes clear. Their mission is to take Yeshua's message to the nations.

Another obstacle that has the potential to shipwreck the ambitions of the Messianic Gentile involves the concept of obligation to the Torah. Many Messianic Gentiles' first connection point to their Jewish roots is through taking hold of some of the Torah's commandments. Because of this, it may seem like the first angle of approach when communicating one's Jewish roots to his friends and family is to try to convince them that they are fully obligated to the Torah, and that they should begin to observe Sabbath, festivals, and dietary laws right away or face judgment.

This approach is also doomed to failure. Not only is the New Testament perfectly clear that this is not the case; most of the verses that articulate this fact are among the most popular and well-known verses in the Bible. As you know if you grew up in a Christian environment, Christians know and are taught from a young age that the apostles did not bind Gentile believers to the entire Mosaic Law as such.

And while this idea must be heavily qualified due to the specific obligations the apostles *did* place on Gentile believers, it is correct to say that Christians have no divine mandate to be fully Torah observant—and Christians, for the most part, know this. To try to convince a Christian that he is under judgment for not wearing tzitzit is futile. It is likely to provoke anger and incredulity proportionate to the level of knowledge he or she has.

In fact, as I mentioned in the last chapter, ninety-nine percent of the time it is not proper for a Messianic Gentile to claim that he or she is personally Torah observant, either. Torah observance—*shomer mitzvot* ("protecting the commandments")—is a well-understood concept in Judaism and involves guarding the commandments as they have been traditionally interpreted. Claiming to keep the commandments while ignoring the traditional method of their observance is misleading at best.

An outstanding example is Sabbath observance (*shomer Shabbat*). A Messianic Gentile who has recently taken hold of the beauty of the Sabbath rest might be tempted to say that he is "keeping the Sabbath" or "Sabbath observant." However, to be truly *shomer Shabbat* requires an incredible lifestyle change. It is difficult and demanding for modern families to prepare for a day without electric lights, cooking implements, money, driving, phones, computers, and other modern conveniences. The scope of Sabbath commandments goes far beyond what most Messianic Gentiles would even consider.[53]

For a Messianic Gentile to set aside the traditional understanding of Sabbath observance in Judaism and simultaneously claim to be Sabbath observant is confusing and misleading. Claiming these terms—Torah observant, Sabbath observant—without living up to the standard they represent hurts the character of the claimant and diminishes what those terms mean.

Yet another pitfall is the tendency to enter a church and try to influence the congregants under the nose of the church leadership. Most Christian pastors are very concerned with the spiritual growth of their congregants and go to great lengths to ensure that they are delivering a solid, biblical message. To sneak into a congregation in order to propagate a different message will provoke a nasty response and harden people's hearts to our message.

A similar, equally dangerous route is to establish a congregation solely for the purpose of siphoning members from other churches. While Messianic Gentile congregations are a beautiful and necessary expression of faith, they should be started and maintained by an informed and dedicated group of members who intend to live out the Messianic ideal for its own sake, and not simply in order to try to capture members of other congregations.

In reality, our faith is not about us, our level of observance, our path of discovery, or our journey toward holiness. These are all vitally important concepts, but cannot compare to the work of God through Yeshua the Messiah.

This leads to another difficulty. It is extremely difficult—nearly impossible—to establish a healthy Messianic Gentile congregation in the first place. It can happen, and it can meet with success, particularly if it is established by people who are dedicated to stay connected and under the authority of a Messianic Jewish covering body. But it is usually a losing proposition from the beginning. New congregations, including Messianic Gentile congregations, often attract people who are dissatisfied with their own church leadership or congregational life and are looking for something different. The new atmosphere often does not relieve their dissatisfaction; rather, it is now projected on to the leadership of the new congregation.

Leading a congregation is extremely difficult for a variety of other reasons as well. I have seen far more Messianic Gentile congregations fail than succeed. It is much easier and potentially far more fruitful to remain active in a church that is already grounded and healthy and try to make a positive difference there. When a church becomes open to these concepts, it becomes a venue through which others can be taught, whether in home groups or in a Shabbat Torah study group at the church.

A MORE EXCELLENT WAY

The way of the Messianic Gentile is indeed difficult and marked with significant pitfalls. But don't be discouraged. There is a way to avoid these pitfalls and become *shlichim*, ambassadors for Christ who make peace instead of fomenting discord, who draw people to Torah and Messiah instead of pushing them away.

To become a *shaliach*, one must have a solid point of departure; like a building, the quest to become a *shaliach* must be built on a solid foundation. For all believing Gentiles, Messianic or not, the foundation is the same: Yeshua the Messiah (1 Corinthians 3:11). Yeshua is the believing Gentile's foundation, his only connection point to God, to Israel, and to the Torah.

It should go without saying, but the Messianic Gentile's faith must be Christ-centered, not Torah-centered. The Torah *informs* the Gentile's obligations, but Messiah is the *source of* and *reason for* those obligations. The Torah in apostolic theology is important, but is always relativized in deference to the overwhelming importance of the Messiah. Yeshua and the apostles consistently taught that as beautiful and majestic as the Torah is, Messiah surpasses it and its author, Moses.[54] This idea is found in Jewish sources as well,[55] though Judaism is not monolithic and many divergent views exist.

The centrality and all-encompassing greatness of Messiah is a concept that should unite Messianic Gentiles, Messianic Jews, and mainstream Christians. It should be the common foundation on which we all can build.

Placing and keeping Messiah at the center of one's faith and life is an important inoculation against the tendency to get so caught up in the rediscovery of the Torah's greatness that the centrality of Yeshua is displaced. Keeping Yeshua central is absolutely necessary; at the end of the day, *this is how our faith must operate in order to be biblical*. If we do not internalize the New Testament's own testimony about Yeshua and his proper place as the object, center, author, consummator, and foundation of our faith, then we have all fallen short of the high calling the Father has placed on our lives.

In reality, our faith is not about us, our level of observance, our path of discovery, or our journey toward holiness. These are all vitally important concepts, but cannot compare to the work of God in reconciling humanity to himself and consummating his entire creation through Yeshua the Messiah. As agents, we reflect and represent Yeshua, and we embody his message and his teachings, but this observance is not an end in itself. It is a means to the glorification of God. This realization should inspire humility, deference, conciliation, and peace among all believers.

If Messianic Gentiles completely dedicate themselves to conforming to the image of Messiah for his own sake, and to serving Messiah with every fiber of their being, they will have taken the first step toward being true *shlichim*, faithful representatives of the Messiah.

The next step for a Messianic Gentile, after prioritizing the Messiah, is adopting a coherent identity for himself. It is easy to feel marginalized because of the particular uniqueness of Messianic theology and practice. A Messianic Gentile might feel stuck between Christianity and Judaism. The varying potential solutions to this problem—claiming Jewish identity through Messiah, through being descended from the ten lost tribes,[56] through transfer into a political entity called "Israel"—are inconsistent with the scriptural witness, and inadvertently promote a supersessionist theology in which the distinction and value of being Jewish is erased.

Messianic Gentiles must embrace their identity as believing members of the nations and not conflate their identity with that of the Jewish people. Restoring the Tent of David means recapturing a biblical vision for Jew and Gentile worshiping the God of Israel together without breaking down the distinction between them. As part of the "commonwealth of Israel" (Ephesians 2:12), believing Gentiles have a unique and irrevocable calling of their own.

Knowledgeable Christians have read the New Testament. They know Galatians and Acts and the Gospels and though there are some serious traditional misinterpretations of these texts,[57] traditional Christians understand that unless they are Jews or proselytes, they are not Jewish. The message of the Messianic Gentile must encompass the idea that Gentile believers are important to God as Gentiles, that the existence of millions of believing Gentiles is a fulfillment of biblical prophecy, and that God has always envisioned Gentiles joining themselves to Messiah and to Israel without losing their ethnic identity, language, or national heritage.[58]

Furthermore, understanding one's identity and calling as a Gentile believer is necessary in order for one to truly appreciate the unique calling and destiny of the Jewish people. The Messianic Gentile must always be careful to respect the exclusive, irrevocable calling God has placed on the Jewish people.

The next step toward becoming a *shaliach* is cultivating a heart for others—we must, as Paul wrote, "Let love be genuine" (Romans 12:9). A Jewish proverb states that "what comes from the heart enters the heart." If people sense that someone doesn't truly care about them, they won't listen to what he has to say. The best way to ensure that one's message is accepted by others is to truly love them and prioritize their needs above one's own. In fact, this loving selflessness should be demonstrated toward everyone regardless of the mission outlined in this book.

It is easy to lose focus on the importance of genuine love; it is not hard to redefine love as nothing more than keeping the commandments, on the basis of 1 John 5:3 and similar verses. Yet love is more than that. Love encompasses obedience to God but is not limited to outward observance. Real love comes from the heart; real love is not merely volitional but emotional and spiritual.

Yeshua's entire earthly ministry was characterized by compassion for others. He was busy; he woke up early and stayed up late, and was tired enough to sleep through a thunderstorm on a boat; but when he saw the crowds of people, he had compassion on them and healed their sick (Matthew 9:36, 14:14). He gave up his own comfort in order to make others comfortable. In the end, he gave up his life to save the world, despite having the power to take the world by force. Our lives should—but rarely do—exemplify this same self-sacrificing love and compassion.

It is impossible for a person with any amount of spiritual awareness not to listen to someone who truly loves and cares about them. People want to be appreciated and cared about; fulfilling this need in their life will open the door for real friendship. Real friends will care about your theology and listen to what you have to say. It may sound trite, but this kind of relationship-building is essential in being a disciple among the nations, and it is the best and most sustainable way to spread the message of Yeshua's Jewishness. It has a multiplicative effect as well; making others into *shlichim* of the Messiah is one of the most effective ways to use our time and effort. In fact, it is one of the highest callings our Master gave us.

Hand-in-hand with this concept of love and self-sacrifice is the important idea that Messianic Gentiles must be willing to compromise in gray areas in order to accommodate others. Messianic Jewish Rabbi David Rudolph's doctoral dissertation, *A Jew to the Jews*,[59]

Real friends will care about your theology
and listen to what you have to say.
Relationship-building is the best and
most sustainable way to spread the
message of Yeshua's Jewishness.

analyzes Paul's philosophy of accommodation in 1 Corinthians
9:19–23. Paul wrote to the Corinthians that he became "all things
to all men." Rudolph points out that this passage has been misin-
terpreted to mean that Paul discarded the Mosaic Law in order to
accommodate Gentiles. Yet it is clear according to Rudolph's analysis
that there were some stringencies Paul was willing to relax in order
to be able to have table fellowship with Gentile believers.

Paul remained a Torah-observant Jew throughout his life. Yet
he had no problem ministering to Jews and Gentiles. He could fellowship, worship, and eat with both groups because he was willing
to place his personal priorities aside for the sake of others. If the
Apostle Paul, a great tzaddik, could adopt this kind of conciliatory,
deferential attitude, how much more should Messianic Gentiles be
willing to humble themselves in order to accommodate other Christians—especially considering the fact that they are not obligated to
many of the commandments!

New First Fruits of Zion staff members are often encouraged to
read a book called *The Rebbe's Army*, by Sue Fishkoff.[60] *The Rebbe's
Army* is an in-depth analysis of the Chabad-Lubavitch movement,
a Chasidic sect famous for organizing giant menorah lightings and
other conspicuous forms of Jewish outreach.

Chabad also calls its emissaries *shlichim*. The lengths to which these young couples go in order to bring the message of chasidism to secular Jews are amazing. They leave the religious community behind and have to fend for themselves. They receive a small stipend for the beginning stages of their outreach and are expected to raise their own funds thereafter. Going door-to-door, organizing parties on the biblical feast days, making lots of phone calls, and generally being as friendly and accommodating as possible, these *shlichim* have had enormous success in popularizing Chabad chasidism.

Yet all the while, they retain their high level of Torah observance. Chabad chasidim are very stringent in many areas. They are restricted to *chalav yisrael*, dairy products that are produced exclusively under Jewish supervision. They dress with a very high level of modesty. And yet their outreach has been tremendously effective, despite the restrictions and difficulties of living an observant lifestyle outside a religious Jewish community. This is largely because of their undying devotion to their rebbe, Menachem Mendel Schneerson.

Chabad *shlichim* feel that the rebbe is always watching over them, empowering them to continue spreading the message of *Chasidut*, even though he passed away in 1994 and a successor was never appointed. Their intense drive to continue propagating Rabbi Schneerson's message is tied to their love for him personally.

Chabad *shlichim* go to great lengths to bring Chabad's message to other Jews, even in remote locations where there are few Jews to be found. To them, leaving the relatively comfortable, insular Chabad community in New York for a distant land is all worth it even if only one Jew responds positively.

Think of the multitudes of Jews and Gentiles who attend traditional churches. What an incredible opportunity exists at the doorstep of the Messianic Gentile who reengages the church! The Chabad *shlichim* will go thousands of miles for one Jew; depending on where he lives, the Messianic Gentile may only have to go a few miles to potentially impact thousands of believing Jews and non-Jewish Christians.

Seeing what Chabad has been able to do under challenging circumstances and with all the restrictions of an observant lifestyle is at once inspiring and depressing. On one hand, it is amazing to see that it can be done—sincere devotion to our rabbi, Yeshua, can inspire us to do great things for him without having to compromise our observance. On the other hand, the Messianic movement has not even come close to replicating the success of Chabad chasidism—and our rabbi *is* the Messiah!

Though the Jewish roots movement has made great strides, Messianic Gentiles have yet to gain the kind of widespread acceptance and success that one would expect, given the biblical nature and prophetic destiny of their message. They have barely touched the millions of Gentiles and hundreds of thousands of Jews waiting in churches to hear the message of Yeshua's Jewishness. So much more needs to be done.

The mission to change the church and wake Christians up to the reality of the Jewish roots of their faith is the perfect opportunity to get up and do something for Messiah. Yet there are some careful guidelines that must be followed in order for this mission to be successful.

WHAT A SHALIACH IS NOT[61]

◊ A *shaliach* is not someone who focuses on the faults of others, to the exclusion of his own.

◊ A *shaliach* is not looking to catch someone else in sin, hoping for the opportunity to bring correction.

◊ A *shaliach* is not someone who only associates with people who think, believe, and act like him, while lambasting everyone who disagrees with him.

◊ A *shaliach*'s defining quality is not what he defines himself against; he is not better known for what he is against than what he is for.

◊ A *shaliach* is not proud or boastful of the knowledge he has that others do not.

◊ A *shaliach* is not dismissive of the movement of God in the lives of other people, even when it doesn't look exactly the way he thinks it should.

◊ A *shaliach* does not falsely accuse those with whom he disagrees of moral or intellectual failings.

WHAT A SHALIACH IS

◊ A *shaliach* is someone who is conformed by the image of Messiah and deeply desires to reveal his life through the life of the *shaliach*.[62]

◊ A *shaliach* is someone who is poor in spirit, humble, who hungers and thirsts for righteousness, is compassionate, pure in heart, a pursuer of shalom, one who takes insult, and endures difficulty—for his is the kingdom of heaven.[63]

◊ A *shaliach* is someone who will strive to outdo others in showing honor.[64]

◊ A *shaliach* is someone who steps out of his comfort zone to connect with individuals with different values.[65]

A *shaliach* teaches by example, holding himself to a high standard rather than projecting that standard onto others.[66]

.

More than a Mission

—––◇◇◇––—

This sounds fishy. Is it really okay
to go to church in order to change
the beliefs of the people there?

B efore we go on, a reminder: being a *shaliach* isn't easy. It's also not for everyone. Some Messianic Gentiles are connected with solid Messianic Jewish communities—that is, healthy communities which have positive relationships with local churches and which do not define themselves against the church. In no way are we encouraging Messianic Gentiles to leave these communities behind.

Stable Messianic Jewish congregations can be a wonderful place for Messianic Gentiles to live out their faith, if they are truly committed to the mission of the congregation and willing to submit to its leadership. They can certainly benefit from the broad vision of this book, but they are probably not called to the specific mission outlined in it. Rather, their role in restoring the Tent of David is to work closely with Messianic Jews to restore and build up Messianic Judaism as a viable, sustainable faith tradition.

This book is primarily written for non-Jewish Christians who are or have been connected with a local church and who are looking for a way to positively contribute to the establishment of the Tent of David.

In our *HaYesod* program, a ten-week study on the Jewish foundations of Christianity, we recommend that Gentile believers who tap into their spiritual heritage in Judaism should retain their connections with the broader Christian community, and specifically with a local church.

One *HaYesod* student, Linda, recently emailed me with the difficulty she has experienced in this situation:

> I have just finished your *HaYesod* course and have heard
> Boaz, Daniel, and Toby all say that we, as Christians,
> should stay connected with our Christian fellowship
> once we have begun the life-changing journey of Messianic Judaism. The problem I have found in doing that

is the messages on Sunday morning contain teachings contrary to what I have learned on my journey thus far. Do you have any suggestions in how to deal with this? I dearly love the people there but find I constantly have to sift through everything that is taught and I come home frustrated. Any suggestions on how to deal with this would really be appreciated.

Those who put into action the mission of this book are likely to find themselves at the same crossroads as Linda. As someone who has put this mission into practice, I understand the frustration and concern that can accompany it.

However, I also see the immense potential for growth and change that Messianic Gentiles can have, if they commit to joining or remaining part of their local churches. I believe God has a job for them to do.

To Linda and those like her, I say—hang in there. God has given you the understanding you have. He has put you exactly where he wants you. He desires for the whole body of Messiah to hear this message, to hear the authentic gospel of Yeshua the Messiah in its original Jewish context. Without you, without *shlichim*, this will never happen.

This book is intended to help you along the way. As such, we are about to launch into a practical explanation of exactly how to undertake the mission of strengthening Christianity by reconnecting Christians with their Jewish roots. As I have repeatedly stated, my proposed mission is intended to strengthen the church, not to tear it down, and in the next chapter, I am going to recommend maintaining your connection with a local church—for your sake, for the church's sake, and for the sake of Israel. However, as laudable as the mission outlined in this book is, the mission itself is an extremely poor justification if it's your only reason for going to church.

In the following paragraphs, please forgive my forthrightness; I just need to be fundamentally clear.

To attend a church solely in order to change that church, in order to change the beliefs of the people there, in order to push your own agenda, is unethical. It's wrong. It will be perceived as underhanded and dirty, and it reflects extremely poorly on the entire Messianic Jewish movement. It is more likely to make people despise you and what you stand for than it is to bring them to see your point of view. This approach will harm the mission. It hurts our message and marginalizes its ability to be heard and received.

It's not hard to see why. When someone attends church and claims to be a believer, a certain set of assumptions exists in the minds of the congregants and leadership there. They will assume that their fellow congregant is on board with the basic Christian message, that he is going to help the church accomplish its mission, and that he will submit to the vision of the church and its leadership.

If it were to be made known that, for example, someone in the church was really a Mormon or a Muslim whose sole aim was to convert members of that church to his religion or sect, he would quickly find himself *persona non grata*. Proselytizing others is simply not an appropriate reason to go to church. It is usurping the institution for personal ends. It is a waste of other people's time, energy, and resources.

One who seeks to bring the message of the Jewish roots of the Christian faith into his church in such an underhanded manner will be perceived the same way as a proselytizer of another religion. This may not be how many potential *shlichim* see themselves, and it may not accurately describe what they are trying to do, but this is how they will be perceived, and they will be rejected. If someone tried something similar in your faith community, you would reject them as well.

You may feel like this mission is so important, so right, that the ends justify the means. But they don't. It has to be done right, or it shouldn't be done at all.

To attend a church solely in order to change that church,
in order to change the beliefs of the people there, in
order to push your own agenda, is unethical. It's wrong.

At this point, you may feel as if I've built you up only to tear you down. Rest assured, this isn't the case. However, before moving forward, we must set the mission in its proper context—in the larger world of church, community, family, and faith.

Many Messianic Gentiles feel that they have come a long way forward from where they used to be. To them, their observance of more of the Torah's commandments, their understanding of their Jewish roots, and the various other steps they have taken have set them apart from the broader Christian community in a positive way. This feeling sometimes causes Messianic Gentiles to question whether they really belong in the church.

The great sage Hillel had this piece of wisdom for his disciples, as recorded in *Pirkei Avot* 2:5: "Do not separate yourself from the community."

As we have already explored in this book, the church is a wonderful vehicle that has brought uncountable numbers of people into the kingdom of God. The church is full of God's people. It is the locus for God's activity among non-Jews—and, for the most part, among believing Jews as well. If we would be honest with ourselves and others, a fair assessment of the church would remind us all of the critical role it has played in our own spiritual awakening and journey. It seems noble and self-sacrificing to leave this community of faith in order to progress further toward what one perceives as the ideal, the best way to practice a biblically grounded faith, the best way to understand the Bible, the best theology. If the church won't change, someone might reason, I will leave and practice what I believe to be correct somewhere else, by myself or in a small group, and God will favor me *because I am right.*

Here's the immediate problem, though: if someone separates himself from the community of faith, and afterward tries to pass along his beliefs to the next generation, his children are not likely to continue what he started. And if no one is there to continue what he started, all the "progress" he made is completely lost. In the end, in the long run, everything he did won't matter, because God's activity on earth is not about the spiritual journey or the level of observance of one single person. It's about saving the entire world and how the body of Messiah as a whole should be carrying out their responsibility toward that end.

We will discuss more about this later, but children who grow up in an extremely isolated faith community, in which there is no social structure to help reinforce their beliefs and religious practices, are prime candidates for assimilation into the broader culture. Parents of older children who leave the church also risk alienating their children and putting a serious roadblock in their spiritual development. The danger is not only that they will reject the theology and practice of the fringe group their parents became a part of. The real danger is that they will reject any form of faith whatsoever.

Why is it so hard to raise a Christian family outside the church? Because God's chosen instrument to represent the Master is not the individual believer so much as the entire community of faith. Consequently, those who have abandoned Christianity are neglecting one of the most basic Scriptural principles: the command to be in fellowship with the broader body of Messiah.

FELLOWSHIP

When one adopts a philosophy that is different from the historically normative theology of the church, it becomes especially important for that person to remember that the community of faith remains the people of God, whether it is right or wrong about a certain issue, and whether it is corporately being obedient or disobedient. For example, Israel and Judah remained God's people even when they walked in abject apostasy, worshipping others gods and sacrificing to idols. "The gifts and the calling of God are irrevocable" (Romans 11:29). It is on this basis that we can declare today that Jews who do not believe in Yeshua are still God's people. In the same way, mainstream Christians are still God's people, even if they have generally rejected the Jewish people as God's continuing covenant people and the Torah as God's blueprint of faith for the Jewish people.

As such, the Messianic Gentile need have no fear of joining together with this broader corporate body, even if he cannot in good conscience advocate every single thing that comes from the pulpit. Suitable analogies can be drawn from both Yeshua and Paul. In instructing his disciples how they related to the spiritual leaders of the Jewish people, the scribes and Pharisees, Yeshua admonished them to follow their teachings, though he excoriated them for their hypocrisy and their failure to live up to the standard they set for themselves and others (Matthew 23, esp. verses 2–3).

Similarly, Paul, before the Sanhedrin, challenged the priesthood directly and stood for what he believed in. Yet, when he realized that he had personally insulted the high priest, Ananias, he apologized and even repented. Paul still recognized the authority of the Sanhedrin and the priesthood, even though he remained firm in his convictions.

Living out one's salvation is not primarily about what we know, or how much we know ... It is about being part of the people of God—in our case, as believers, we are the body of Messiah.

In the same way, the Messianic Gentile can affiliate himself with a church, submit to its leadership, and assimilate into the body of believers without giving up his convictions about the Jewish roots of the Christian faith. Even the challenges one *does* have to endure in order to maintain a harmonious relationship with the church are worth the reward—because being right about everything is not what gets a believer in God's good graces.

Living out one's salvation is not primarily about what we know, or how much we know (though obviously there is a baseline level of knowledge that is required to understand God's message of salvation). It is about being part of the people of God—in our case, as believers, we are the body of Messiah. Cutting oneself off from this body—and from a physical, stable, visible expression of faith that is recognized by this body—can only lead to spiritual decline.

The author of Hebrews, recognizing this danger, exhorted his community in Hebrews 10:19–25:

Therefore, brothers, since we have confidence to enter
the holy places by the blood of Jesus, by the new and
living way that he opened for us through the curtain,
that is, through his flesh, and since we have a great
priest over the house of God, let us draw near with a
true heart in full assurance of faith, with our hearts
sprinkled clean from an evil conscience and our bodies
washed with pure water. *Let us hold fast the confession
of our hope without wavering*, for he who promised is
faithful. And *let us consider how to stir up one another
to love and good works*, not *neglecting to meet together*,
as is the habit of some, but encouraging one another,
and all the more as you see the Day drawing near.

The last sentence of this passage brings out the author's clear
intent for his community. In plain language, he states what he has
hinted at in other sections of his sermon: he desires for his community to continue meeting together as one group, in spite of the
difficulties they are facing.

First he exhorts them to draw near, as a unified community, to
God, vividly described as dwelling in the holy place in the heavenly
Temple. This language recalls the Temple service, in which the
entire Jewish nation either gathered at the Temple or stopped what
they were doing to pray at the time of the twice-daily *tamid* offer-
ing. Through these oft-repeated prayers, even after the Temple was
destroyed, the Jewish people continued (and still continue) to be
bound together in worship.

Hebrews' author then pleads with his audience to hold fast
to their confession of hope—which, in light of his next sentence,
directly implies holding fast to the community which shares that
confession. In the mind of the author of Hebrews, the confession of

faith in Yeshua as the Messiah is like glue, holding the community together as one.

This is why, immediately afterward, the author of Hebrews encourages his audience to stir one another up to good works. Rather than allow them to attempt to keep the faith alone, he knows that the life of faith only works when believers are there to encourage each other to do what is right. So finally, he plainly asks his congregation not to neglect meeting together regularly. It is this venue—the local assembly (i.e., "the church," if you will)—that he envisions as the primary place and mode of connection for believers.

Without a solid, stable community of faith, believers languish. Without the accountability and encouragement that a grounded community brings, families struggle to maintain a healthy, balanced life of faith. This is not to say that home churches or small unaffiliated faith communities are not legitimate. However, these communities are more susceptible to be deprived of structured, trained leadership; a steady and balanced theological foundation; and the resources to help children grow up with a balanced and measured view of their faith and how they relate to the world.

Perhaps this does not describe your personal situation. Perhaps you are one of the few Messianic Gentiles who has found fellowship in a stable, healthy, Messianic Jewish congregation. If so, I encourage you to stay there, where God has planted you, and contribute toward the success of your community. Support the leadership and realize that you are fortunate to be part of a solid, Messianic congregation. Most Messianic Gentiles do not share your good fortune.

I commend to those Messianic Gentiles who have not found such a congregation the necessity of belonging to a local church. In reality, the party which has the potential to benefit most is not the local church, which may have a few theological problems. The primary beneficiary is the Messianic Gentile, who otherwise risks being deprived of the joy of participating in worship with his fellow believers in the context of a healthy, grounded community.

The practical advice in the next chapter is geared toward the accomplishment of the mission this book is all about—returning Christianity to its Jewish roots. But this is not the primary reason a Messianic Gentile should consider retaining a strong connection to a local church. Rather, he should be part of a local, stable body of believers and submit himself to the rule of that community because that is how Yeshua has commanded his assembly to operate. We are not single, isolated shining stars, nor are we lone voices in the wilderness. We are, by definition, part of something much bigger—a movement of God that dwarfs our individual distinctiveness, differences, and peculiarities. It is therefore our responsibility as believers to live and operate in solidarity with other believers and embrace our role as part of this greater movement—part of broader Christianity.

As part of a local church, in most cases, you can still be who you are—someone who is honestly and openly exploring the Jewish roots of your faith. But Messianic Gentiles must beware of the idea that they are something better or superior to non-Messianic Christians, and recognize their place as part of the body of Messiah, part of the organized local church, not because they feel they are in a position to change its theology, but because, for the most part, they simply belong there.

Good churches are the place for connection, growth, support, and a shared collective effort of outreach to the hurting surrounding community. There is strength in numbers; groups of dedicated people have far more power to change the world than individuals. The Messianic Gentile needs to be one of those people, part of something bigger than himself.

FAMILY

I mentioned above the danger of raising believing children outside of the context of a local church. I believe—and this belief has been repeatedly confirmed as I hear the experiences of others—that the existence of a solid community of faith is absolutely necessary in order to provide an environment where children can grow up equipped to carry their faith forward to the next generation. A single family is rarely able to provide that environment all by itself.

Feeling like they are not part of something bigger and more organized is enough to cause a teenager to reconsider the viability of their whole belief system. They may feel unequipped to survive in the world or to live out their faith. They may not feel like their faith rests on a sure foundation. They may feel isolated and consequently their potential is limited.

In contrast, the children of a Messianic Gentile have the potential to thrive in a healthy church, being given a solid identity as a non-Jewish believer in Yeshua and a solid social framework within which to live out that identity.

The generation of teenagers and young adults currently poised to take an active role in building the next generation's spiritual communities are more interconnected and globally minded than their parents are. They are far more likely to tap into a bigger, more universal view of what religion and faith is all about than they are to continue in what they will likely perceive—correctly or incorrectly—as an irrelevant fringe group.

Many deeply pious people have reacted against this young generation's approach to faith, rejecting the idea that all of God's people should be able to come together in spite of their differences. To them, their own dogmas and particular theologies are God-revealed truth, and every other church and denomination is held in the grip of error, waiting to be judged. Messianic Gentiles are not immune from this kind of dogmatic mindset.

But our children, by and large, are not growing up with this narrow, fundamentalist mindset at all. As someone who was born right on the top edge of Generation X, I have watched today's young people—my own children included—embrace a totally different approach to their faith. They want to be part of something bigger. They want to change the world for the better, and they understand that to do that, they can't waste energy fighting other believers. So instead of primarily identifying themselves as holding a particular theology, they are mission-driven. Their desire to make the world a better place in the name of our Master, rather than their adherence to an intellectual definition of faith, is what defines them.

My children have grown up with this sense of mission, and I have helped to cultivate it in their lives because I believe that mission is stronger than theology. Mission will continue to drive and define people even when their theology is under attack. Mission can cause people to work together who will never agree on theological issues. I believe that my children will be able to survive in this present world and work together with any of God's people because they are defined by their mission to bring the kingdom of God into the world.

In a way, this mission-oriented mindset is what defined the early church as well. The first followers of Yeshua didn't sit down and write creeds and statements of faith the day after Yeshua returned to the Father. Rather, they immediately began to implement the Master's plan of action to spread the kingdom of God throughout the world (first to the Jewish people, and later, after God's revelation to Peter, to the Gentiles).

This is not to say that theology isn't important. It is important. The Bible is full of theology and theological statements. However, differing interpretations of these statements should not present an impassible barrier between those who share the same simple confession of faith in Yeshua as the Messiah of Israel and the Son of God. The shared mission is simply more important.

One might wonder whether their children will lose their identity as Messianic Gentiles in a local church environment. This objection is more fully answered in the next chapter. However, by instilling in their children a sense of mission, bringing them up to be wholehearted followers of Yeshua, and giving them a secure place (the church) to practice their faith alongside their peers, the Messianic Gentile will potentially save their children a great deal of bitterness, heartache, and resentment, and their faith will, in the end, be stronger.

Furthermore, they may even have a greater impact within the church than their parents can, as their Christian friends will be impressed with the social, practical, and deeply spiritual life a Messianic expression of faith and understanding represents. Since this mission is inter-generational, the impact these young people have the potential to make in this simple, organic way cannot be underestimated.

The potential benefit to one's family as a result of joining a healthy church is not limited to children, either. It is not unheard of for marriages to fall apart and families to divide after leaving the church behind. Without the accountability and help that can come from a larger body of believers, many marriages dissolve that otherwise may have flourished. It goes without saying that children in such families do not often come to share their parents' perspective on spirituality.

This is not to say that these problems don't also exist within the church. No church is perfect and many families within the church find their problems impossible to deal with productively. Many churches struggle to fill their congregation's need for the kind of support network that helps families stay together. However, in healthy churches there is at least the potential for the community to rally around a troubled family and give them the resources and support they need.

THE SHALIACH'S CALLING

We have established that for the sake of fellowship and for the health of his family, the Messianic Gentile should seriously consider remaining connected with his local church. After these two reasons, the mission outlined in this book—returning Christianity to its Jewish roots—is a distant third.

At this point it may be helpful to introduce the concept of mixed motives. At the beginning of this chapter I affirmed that going to church solely in order to bring people into an understanding of their Jewish roots is unethical. Yet throughout this book I encourage people to go to church and to bring other Christians to an understanding of their Jewish roots.

If we were to be honest with ourselves, we hardly ever do anything for one single reason. For example, we eat because we are hungry, but we also eat because the food we are eating tastes good. If we are very hungry, we will eat stale bread. But if given a choice, we would rather have something delectable.

Where we get into trouble is when we eat just to eat—when we don't need nourishment but we overindulge because the food tastes good. At this point our motives have been corrupted and we are being purely gluttonous and selfish.

In the same way, if a Messianic Gentile approaches the idea of going to church as a means to an end, where the end is to cause other

Christians to become Messianic Gentiles, he is in danger of unethically subverting the church to his own ends. On the other hand, if his primary motive is to support the church for its own sake, and the mission to spread the knowledge of Christianity's Jewish roots is a secondary motive, he is on firmer ground.

After all, if you are a Messianic Gentile, chances are that this mission is an important and defining aspect of your life. We all long to see a genuine, apostolic form of worship restored.

Most Messianic Gentiles, at first, long to see this restoration happen in the church. They can feel the massive potential for positive change—really, revival—in the church, and they hope their families, friends, and fellow congregants will immediately catch their vision. Unfortunately, after a few roadblocks, it is easy to become disillusioned and to begin to see the church as an enemy rather than a friend, and a battleground instead of a home.

The best way for the Messianic Gentile to avoid this disillusionment and retain the passion he had when he first discovered his Jewish roots is to fall in love with the spiritual future of the church. He must see it in its full beauty. He must imagine what he wants the church to look like, envision it, and then work to make it a reality. The Messianic Gentile should invest in the church because he believes in it, because he sees its potential, and because he is able, through love, to overlook its flaws.

Just as in any marriage where a husband and wife may disagree or even fight, and yet still love each other and be committed to each other, the Messianic Gentile will not always find that things in church go exactly as he plans. However, if he is truly invested in the church and loves the people there and the body of believers with whom he has joined himself, he is able to look past or work through problems productively.

The Messianic Gentile should invest in the church
because he believes in it, because he sees its potential,
and because he is able, through love, to overlook its flaws.

To successfully view the mission this way, though, one must truly be invested in his church at all levels. For the Messianic Gentile who has chosen to join a local church, "the church I go to" will become "my church"; "the pastor" will become "my pastor." The desire to see positive change, reform, and revival in the church must be born of a genuine love and concern for the people there. Just as importantly, this desire must also be pursued in concert and consultation with the pastoral staff, the lay leadership, and the mission and vision of the church.

The Messianic Gentile must constantly reevaluate his motivations for attending a local church. He must keep in mind the ethical issues this mission entails as he approaches each decision he makes. Does he see himself as a covert agent, secretly slipping in a message that is not welcome at the church? If so, it is time to take a step back and reconsider. However, if he can honestly say that he has accepted the church as it is, and that he is willing to throw his lot in with other believers in solidarity with the greater body of Messiah, for better or for worse, then he is beginning to cultivate the kind of attitude and ethic required to make a positive contribution, over time, to a local church.

Consider Peter's words in his second epistle (2 Peter 1:3–15):

> His divine power has granted to us all things that
> pertain to life and godliness, through the knowledge
> of him who called us to his own glory and excellence,

by which he has granted to us his precious and very great promises, so that through them you may become partakers of the divine nature, having escaped from the corruption that is in the world because of sinful desire.

For this very reason, make every effort to supplement your faith with virtue, and virtue with knowledge, and knowledge with self-control, and self-control with steadfastness, and steadfastness with godliness, and godliness with brotherly affection, and brotherly affection with love.

For if these qualities are yours and are increasing, they keep you from being ineffective or unfruitful in the knowledge of our Lord Jesus Christ. For whoever lacks these qualities is so nearsighted that he is blind, having forgotten that he was cleansed from his former sins. Therefore, brothers, be all the more diligent to confirm your calling and election, for if you practice these qualities you will never fall. For in this way there will be richly provided for you an entrance into the eternal kingdom of our Lord and Savior Jesus Christ.

Therefore I intend always to remind you of these qualities, though you know them and are established in the truth that you have. I think it right, as long as I am in this body, to stir you up by way of reminder, since I know that the putting off of my body will be soon, as our Lord Jesus Christ made clear to me. And I will make every effort so that after my departure you may be able at any time to recall these things.

It is easy to gloss over the list of essential character traits Peter provides for his audience. This is unfortunate, as many believers are struggling to make it past the first—"faith." For too many, these character traits are absent or lacking, leaving severe blind spots that will hamper their ability to take up the mission of this book in an ethical, blameless way. The lack of attention to character development thus renders many ineffective in the kingdom.

The Messianic Gentile must have faith—faith in God, and in God's promise to redeem the nations. He must have faith that regardless of what he is able to personally contribute to the mission, God is ultimately in control and will honor the effort of a pure heart. He must trust that God is watching over him and will bless his honest efforts born from pure motives.

Likewise, virtue: the Messianic Gentile must constantly have an eye toward ethics—toward the way he interacts with, presents himself to, and influences the world on all levels. He must live in such a way that he can be "approved by men" (Romans 14:18), "live peaceably with all" (Romans 12:18), and "taking pains to do what is right, not only in the eyes of the Lord but also in the eyes of men" (2 Corinthians 18:21). All of the Messianic Gentile's interactions with others must be above reproach and unquestionably virtuous. The complex and robust discipline of *mussar* can be extremely helpful to this end.

Knowledge—for "by wisdom a house is built, and by understanding it is established; by knowledge the rooms are filled with all precious and pleasant riches. A wise man is full of strength, and a man of knowledge enhances his might" (Proverbs 24:3–5). The Messianic Gentile must know what he is talking about and be able to accurately define and defend his beliefs in such a way that he does not come off as abrasive or haughty, but as competent, confident, able, and humble.

The Messianic Gentile must develop self-control, the ability to hold his tongue, to refrain from unprofitable arguments. He cannot be quick to anger. He must demonstrate equanimity—the ability to weather any situation without losing his temper, becoming depressed, or developing an inflated sense of self-importance.

Next is steadfastness. The Messianic Gentile must "stand firm in the Lord" (Philippians 4:1), not allowing circumstances to keep him from pressing on toward his goal. Gently but firmly, he must stick to his convictions, and be able to explain why he believes what he believes without deprecating others.

The Messianic Gentile must develop self-control, the ability to hold his tongue, to refrain from unprofitable arguments. He cannot be quick to anger.

This leads to godliness—imitation of God, taking on God's own attributes and displaying them to the world. As "it is proper for man to imitate his Creator" (the opening sentence of *Tomer Devorah*), the Messianic Gentile must exemplify the divine nature in all of his dealings with others and in his own life of personal piety.

Following this is brotherly affection, which leads directly to love. The implication is that only when one has the attribute of godliness, and can truly see others as God sees them, can one truly begin to develop a deep-seated, genuine, unconditional affection and love for other believers. As the apostle John wrote (1 John 5:1), "everyone who loves the Father loves whoever has been born of him."

In my return to the church, I have slowly grown and developed relationships with my fellow congregants. Those relationships are more important to me than my mission within my church. Those relationships will remain despite the acceptance or rejection of my views. I value the people in my church; I support the church in its efforts to help those in need, to awaken the lost to Messiah, to live lives of value and purpose. I can and do appreciate my church for what it is and for what it is doing. All the while, my message is being accepted and my mission is intact. We have been able to encourage the church to take a trip to Israel, I am leading a Torah study on Wednesday nights, and there is another study called "*Devarim*" (Deuteronomy) on Sunday nights—one that I didn't start, nor do I lead.

Things at the church are changing—and I am one of those things. I now have a pastor and a friend who is faithful to have coffee with me each Wednesday morning. I have prayer support for my family and the work of First Fruits of Zion. The church has been there for me, whether it's an electrician who will come to my house at a moment's notice when the power randomly goes out before Shabbat, another guy who fixes my plumbing, or yet another who lets me take his motorcycle out for an afternoon of fun and relaxation. I value the people of my church because they are the people of God; they are my brothers and sisters in Messiah; they are family. I need them and they need me.

This genuine love for others should direct the actions and attitudes of the Messianic Gentile as he builds and maintains relationships within the church. It is impossible to succeed in this mission if it is undertaken purely for its own sake, as an abstract idea, as something more important than the very people whose lives it will strengthen, change, and mold. In the end, it must be undertaken out of love and genuine concern for others—the kind of love that manifests as one joins together with the rest of the body of Messiah.

Restoring the Tent of David

So you want to change the world?
Here's how—you can start today.

Messianic Gentiles have an incredible opportunity to make a difference—to transform their world for the good of Israel and for the sake of Christianity. They have been given a great gift: the gift of understanding Yeshua in his Jewish context, of seeing the greatness of the Torah, a love for Israel, for the Jewish people, and a renewed zeal for the Gospel. With this gift comes the responsibility of sharing it with others.

We have already discussed that it takes a special kind of person to do this—someone warm, loving, accommodating, gracious, and patient; someone who is fully centered on Messiah and has a strong self-identity as a Christian and a Messianic Gentile; someone who sacrifices their own desires for others and the kingdom of heaven. Every non-Jewish believer should aspire to be such a person.

We have also discussed that this mission must be undertaken with the utmost sensitivity toward the ethical issues involved. One cannot spread the message of Christianity's Jewish roots in a way that is anything less than completely blameless, above-board, and respectful to the church and its leadership.

Believing Gentiles who embrace the Messianic ideal must take seriously the mission of restoring David's fallen tent, of bringing people to Yeshua the Jewish Messiah. It is not an easy mission and in all probability, it will bring some degree of hardship to those who undertake it. Yet one must keep in mind that God's kingdom will encompass the whole earth, and he has delegated the responsibility of spreading the message of that kingdom to his followers.

Furthermore, change may not happen right away. It may take years or decades to see any kind of positive reaction to the message of Yeshua's Jewishness and the continuing relevance of Israel and the Torah. Yet the *shlichim* of Messiah must keep a long view, understanding that their efforts are paving the way for a new wave of understanding and passion for the mission to which Yeshua has called his disciples.

Avot d'Rabbi Natan contains the following story about the famous sage, Rabbi Akiva:

> What was the beginning of Rabbi Akiva? At the age of forty, he had learned no Torah whatsoever. Once, while standing next to a well, he asked, "Who chiseled this stone?" They responded to him, "The water that continuously falls on it every day." Immediately, Rabbi Akiva made a logical deduction and applied it to his own situation: "If that which is soft carves into that which is hard, then all the more so, the words of Torah, which are as hard as iron, will penetrate into my heart, which is flesh and blood!" Immediately, he returned to study Torah.[67]

What Rabbi Akiva discovered is that continual exposure to the Torah over time can effect real change. It may be difficult and it will require patience, but the mission of returning Christianity to its Jewish roots is worth the effort.

Perhaps you are a Messianic Gentile and you have read this far but are not yet convinced that it is your calling to remain in the church and bear gentle witness to the concepts outlined in this book. That is entirely possible. Perhaps God has not called you to this mission. There are certainly Messianic Gentiles who are called to join together with Messianic Jews in establishing congregations that reflect historically and scripturally genuine Messianic Jewish observance. You might be called to help establish a Messianic community, and we desperately need strong, healthy, vibrant Messianic congregations.

But please consider the possibility that you are called to become a *shaliach*. Don't make the decision based on feelings. Instead, meditate on the fact that *someone must go*, that the mission is woefully understaffed, and that you probably already have all of the knowledge and tools necessary to undertake it where God has already placed you, to reach those God has put in your life.

Christianity is, has been, and will always be the locus for believing Gentiles. Engaging Christianity will in almost every case be a far better use of time and resources than trying to build an entirely separate edifice or plant a new kind of church, as Christians are already interested in the Scriptures and already have a connection to Yeshua.

The message of the Messianic Gentile is nothing more and nothing less than genuine, biblically based Christianity. The prophetic destiny of Gentile believers is to be part of the restored Tent of David, to recognize their Jewish king and to conform their lives to the Messianic ideal. The truth will be accepted; it is only a matter of time and effort.

It is entirely possible that in addition to doing great things for the kingdom, Messianic Gentiles will personally benefit from a positive relationship with the local church. The community of believers brings accountability and friendship. Pooling resources helps small groups do bigger things than individuals can. Furthermore, continued exposure to traditional Christian beliefs and doctrines is a healthy learning experience; the increased breadth of knowledge it provides will help Messianic Gentiles to communicate and contextualize their message in a balanced way.

Yet this mission, with all its potential, is not without its dangers. I hope in this chapter to give some concrete advice for those who are being called to engage their churches with the message of Yeshua's Jewishness.

A POSITIVE CONCEPT

Before delving into practical advice, let me introduce an important concept that we believe every Messianic Gentile should adopt, especially before trying to take on the mission outlined in this book. One of the easiest ways to turn Christians off to the message of Christianity's Jewish roots is to present the idea of obligation to the commandments of Torah as the primary platform on which one bases the rest of his message.

There are several reasons not to begin an exploration of one's Jewish roots with this idea. First, it is primarily taken as a negative message—"You're not doing something you're supposed to be doing"—and people tend to get defensive in the face of a negative message. Second, it is theologically unsound and most Christians know better than to think they need to be circumcised and obey the dietary laws.

First Fruits of Zion teaches a distinction between the obligations of a Jewish believer and the obligations of a Gentile believer.[68] Not all the commandments that apply to Jews equally apply to Gentiles. This means that Gentile believers who have not taken on those commandments of the Torah that do not pertain to them specifically as Gentiles are not wallowing in sin or rebelling against God. They might be missing out on the disciplines and godly intentions of these commandments, which bring great structure and blessing to one's life—but they are not living in defiance and rebellion towards God.

Gentile Christians are not, in fact, obligated to all of the commandments of the Torah. The apostles chose not to obligate the Gentile believers to certain "sign" commandments and specific markers of Jewish identity which were enjoined specifically upon the physical nation of Israel, the Jewish people: circumcision, Shabbat, festivals, mezuzah, tefillin, tzitzit, kashrut, and the Levitical functions. While

Gentile believers are not disallowed from participation in most of these mitzvot on some level, they do not do so on the same level as a Jewish person's responsibility for covenantal fidelity. Besides, these aspects of Torah can really only be kept properly within the context of a Jewish community and culture.

It is true that traditional Christians have not considered themselves obligated to many of the commandments to which the apostles obligated them.[69] But presenting this failure to obey as the primary platform of our message is still the wrong way to present the beauty and majesty of the Torah. It will usually result in a negative emotional reaction. Instead, we have chosen to make the Jewishness of Yeshua central and build outward from that concept. We feel that this is important for several reasons, not least of which is the fact that *Yeshua is central* to the faith of any Messianic believer, whether Jew or Gentile.

Hand-in-hand with this is the idea of distinction: Gentiles are allowed to take on specifically Jewish aspects of Torah as a way to imitate and connect with the Master, enrich their lives, feed their spiritual development, enhance their understanding of the character of God and of the Scriptures, and show solidarity with the Jewish people.

The *shaliach* must have this attitude toward the mitzvot in order to be able to expect any kind of positive response from other Christians. To reiterate, even mitzvot that Gentile Christians are technically obligated to, such as keeping themselves from meat that has not been properly slaughtered, should be presented gently, and as a positive opportunity to connect with God.

We want to reveal to our brothers and sisters the beauty of the Torah. It represents the opening of new vistas, new understandings. It puts God's spirit as the active force, yet gives the believer an opportunity to respond in love and ability. It is a critically important perspective for anyone who is called to take the message of Christianity's Jewish roots into the church.

BUILDING RELATIONSHIPS

In this chapter we will focus on the particular "do's" and "don'ts" the Messianic Gentile must keep in mind as he seeks to engage other Christians with the message of Christianity's Jewish roots. In order to rebuild the Tent of David, Messianic Gentiles must spread the message of Messiah's inbreaking kingdom to others with special emphasis toward the four distinctive traits of the Messianic faith (Yeshua's Jewishness, the Torah, the gospel, and Israel). This message is biblical and many Christians are ready to accept it. However, there is a right way and a wrong way to try to communicate this message.

Essentially, the right way involves sharing this message in the context of healthy relationships. As we discussed in the previous chapter, building positive relationships with other believers is an end in itself. It is important to remember that befriending other Christians is not just a means to propagating Messianic ideas. We do not advocate the idea of becoming sleeper agents in the church, trying to secretly subvert the institution for your own ends, even if you believe these ends are good.

A relationship predicated on ulterior motives is ultimately destined to fail. It is shallow, meaningless, and manipulative. It is of the utmost importance that Messianic Gentiles develop real, meaningful, unconditional relationships with traditional Christians. The motivation to show people their Jewish Messiah should be a genuine, sincere love for them and a desire to see them grow spiritually for their own sake.

I understand that mixed motives can be an issue here. One might believe he is doing something for the right reason and later discover that he is not so sure anymore. The desire to propagate one's ideas may overwhelm the desire for connection within the body of Messiah, fellowship, and other ethical reasons for wanting to build relationships with other Christians. If at any point someone trying to take on this mission begins to doubt the genuineness of his relationships, the purity of his motives, or the blamelessness of his conduct, he should stop, take a step back, and reconsider. Making friends with any ulterior motive whatsoever will hurt the Messianic Gentile, his testimony, and his message more than almost anything else he can do. It is crass and manipulative. Don't do it!

Assuming it is done for the right reason, building relationships isn't hard. Most of us have been doing it since preschool. However, simply because of the sheer importance of building healthy relationships and the importance of waiting until an appropriate stage to begin sharing one's views with others, I believe it is important to consider the process intentionally and thoughtfully. To that end, in this section we will outline the process of building a successful, healthy, genuine relationship.

To summarize, the four stages of relationship building are: creating rapport, opening dialogue, developing mutual respect, and establishing trust. The process of going through these four stages can take months or even years—it takes time to really get to know someone. Think of how long you have known your closest friends and how long it took you to grow as close as you are.

Chances are, most Messianic Gentiles already have rapport with people in their churches. If they attend regularly, they can probably place names with many of the faces, and vice versa. They have probably engaged many other church members in small talk about various topics. This is a rather benign yet important first stage in the building of strong relationships.

The next phase of relationship building is opening dialogue. Starting conversations with people about more important issues, having deeper conversations, and sharing a little bit of oneself is an experience most churchgoers have frequently.

The next phase is developing mutual respect. As two people grow closer together they begin to think more highly of each other. They may begin to share interests or hobbies that they didn't before. They may visit each other at home and share meals outside of church functions.

The "trust" phase of a relationship is the last phase, in which two people feel very safe with and around each other. People who trust each other might babysit for each other's children or watch each other's homes while the other is away.

This should go without saying, but it is not really appropriate or effective to begin sharing one's deeply held religious convictions in the beginning stages of forming a relationship. That is simply not how relationships work. As people grow closer, this process happens naturally. Don't force it. Make friends because it is the right thing to do, and then let your witness and testimony happen naturally as a part of that friendship.

The fourth phase is the safest time to begin introducing First Fruits of Zion resources to a friend *who is already interested, engaged, and is asking to learn more*. It is overwhelming to be given a book and asked to read it, especially if it contains information that is new and might contradict someone's deeply held beliefs and worldview. So while we certainly recommend First Fruits of Zion resources to help communicate the Messianic message, they must be used thoughtfully and carefully, and are almost always best used in response to a specific question or need raised by the person you are giving the resource to.

Building trusted friends in a local congregation is difficult for some people. Even if you find making friends easy, it still takes time. But remember that your friends have other friends, friends who already trust them and will listen to them. You may only affect one or two people in the church, but they may go on to spread the message further than you could have ever dreamed through their own network of friends and relatives.

As stated above, the easiest way to build trusted Christian friends is simply to stay in church—or, if one has dropped out of church life, to rejoin. However, many Messianic Gentiles have difficulty with this idea, as they find that being different from other believers can cause friction. The next two sections are designed to make church life easier by outlining general principles for accepting and being accepted at a church in spite of the fact that one might not totally agree with traditional Christian theology concerning the Torah and the Jewish people.

HOW TO BE A BLESSING TO THE CHURCH WHILE BEING DIFFERENT

The basic principle of avoiding friction and being a blessing to others at your church—and to the rest of humanity, for that matter—is to judge one's neighbor in righteousness (Leviticus 19:15). Rashi gives an interpretation of this verse that is particularly important and widely accepted in Judaism: "Judge your friend toward the scale of merit [i.e., when the nature of his conduct is questionable, give him the benefit of the doubt]."[70]

In short, to successfully interact with other people, we must assume the best about them. We must judge them favorably. This is an extremely vital lens through which Messianic Gentiles must perceive everyone's words and actions as they participate in church life. If one does not assume the best intentions on the part of his fellow congregants, it will inevitably lead to hurt, distrust, and misunderstanding.

There are several common examples I could use. One is the modern practice of taking communion regularly. Some churches take communion quite often; others take it monthly or quarterly. Yet the institution of the Lord's Supper was in the context of a Seder meal. I believe that yearly, at Passover, is the correct time to observe the commandment of the Lord to break bread and drink wine in remembrance of him.

Yet I do not withdraw from the quarterly communion ceremony at my church. I participate. I overlook the differences I have with the leadership and congregants there, I assume the best about their intentions to honor the Master, and I am not offended at being offered communion outside of a Paschal context.[71] I don't let misunderstandings like this define or mar my relationship with the church.

Leviticus 19:18 commands us not to bear a grudge, but to love others as we want to be loved. It is vital not to bear resentment toward traditional Christians (or toward institutional Christianity, for that matter), but to love them and assume the best about them and their intentions. This mindset is absolutely vital and underlies the rest of the advice I am presenting here.

It is also vitally important to be able to affirm Christianity and what the church is doing. In chapter one, we went over some of the great victories of the church, and established that the church is already striving to obey the weighty matters of the Torah—love, justice, faithfulness. It is important to affirm outwardly and inwardly these positive aspects both of the church as a body and of individuals in the church who are also striving to become better people.

This affirmation manifests in several ways, which will be discussed below. But the first step is an inner realization that the church's stated mission and goal to reach the world for Messiah is intrinsically good and should be pursued. It is important to keep a positive attitude toward the church as an institution in spite of any bad experiences one might have and in spite of the institutional church's historical failures.

More than almost anything else, churches need and appreciate people who are proactively involved. The Messianic Gentile should keep his eyes open for opportunities to join home Bible studies or small groups. He should look for opportunities to volunteer or help. He shouldn't feel like his distinct viewpoint isolates him from other believers. Rather, he should affirm his role as part of the body of Messiah by looking for ways to become more involved at church.

Another important aspect of maintaining one's relationship with a local body of believers is having respect for the church leadership. It is deceptively easy for a Messianic Gentile to feel that his newfound knowledge gives him an interpretive advantage over the church's leadership when it comes to dealing with Scripture. Yet it is vitally important to respect the authority of the church's leadership. When I first began attending the church I am involved with, I did not insert myself into the discussion on the first day of Sunday school. I did not speak or share until I was asked. Still today, I would never share something that I know would undermine the leadership of the church—I am very careful on how I present my views.

Part of this respect is listening and trying to learn from the sermons. As the head of an educational publishing ministry, I have a lot of knowledge about the Bible, but every Sunday, I pay close attention to my pastor's sermon and try to learn whatever I can. Not only that, but I affirm what is good in my pastor's preaching. I always send a note or something to affirm what I learned and what was strong. Only later on, as we got to know each other, did I begin adding small thoughts to give some of the Jewish background of the texts being addressed.

As I look back on the many sermons I have heard, I can't think of one from which I have not gleaned something or had some insight or thought sparked. As stated above, *Pirkei Avot* 6:3 is extremely relevant here. Even if someone only learns one thing from a Christian leader or pastor, it should cause one to develop respect for that person.

Another part of this respect is being candid with the church leadership about one's beliefs and intentions. If the Messianic Gentile is not attending church solely to subvert the institution to his own ends, then he has nothing to hide. Most healthy churches will not kick someone out just for exploring his Jewish roots. In any case, don't pretend to be something you are not; this is disingenuous and will only lead to controversy.

One way to be respectful and implicitly affirm what is good about Christianity is in the simple use of terms. The shift in terminology reflected by the abandonment of the term "Christian" presents an unnecessary barrier. When terms like "Christian," "Jesus," "Christ," and "church" are replaced with Greek or Hebrew synonyms, the traditional Christian feels out of his element, like he is discussing foreign concepts. No matter how much one might try to explain these concepts from a Messianic perspective, the Christian will feel like the Messianic Gentile is pitching a different religion to him.

It is important to keep a conversation with a traditional Christian in traditional terms which everyone understands and can relate to. The Messianic Gentile may, in time, want to introduce concepts that will change the traditional Christian's understanding of terms he is already familiar with, but initially, it is important to frame the discussion in familiar language.

Another aspect of affirming the good in the church is to be positive about the church and its mission. The Messianic Gentile should affirm to himself and others what he holds in common with the church—the kingship of Messiah, a devotion to him and his teachings, a desire to reach the world with his message.

Many churches are struggling financially. If he can, the Messianic Gentile should commit a certain amount of money each week to financially support the church; this gesture will not go unnoticed. Not only does this demonstrate one's affirmation of the church and its mission, it also helps the church to stay solvent. Without local churches, the mission of restoring the apostolic vision would be tremendously more difficult; churches already have much of the infrastructure, resources, and vision required to reach the nations with the message of the kingdom.

Another great way to affirm and get involved with the church is to volunteer, preferably in a non-teaching role at first (unless asked to teach). Most churches, especially smaller ones, rely on volunteers to do yard work, cleaning, maintenance, and other odd jobs. Volunteering to help in these areas is one way to show one's support and willingness to sacrifice his valuable time to support the mission of the church. All of these acts of service help to repair the world; Messianic Gentiles should prioritize these kinds of righteous deeds.

We have already briefly discussed the necessity of being flexible. Supporting an organization like the church means making sacrifices. Maybe Sunday mornings are a convenient time to do yard work. A lot of Christians feel like they are too busy and don't have time to

Whatever you may have to give up to engage
others to strengthen their faith in the
Messiah, it is trivial compared to the reward
waiting for you in the World to Come.

volunteer. In reality, if they were to reprioritize and get rid of things that are less important, most people would be able to make time to help the church out in some way or another.

Remembering what Yeshua and the apostles sacrificed—years and years of dedication, perseverance, and hard work, and in the end, being killed for their beliefs—should inspire us to give up some level of comfort and control in order to be available to God to take on this mission. Whatever you may have to give up in order to be able to engage others to strengthen their faith in the Messiah, it is trivial compared to the reward waiting for you in the World to Come.

Halachic flexibility is another necessity. Becoming a *shaliach* requires one to defer at times to others' idiosyncrasies and foibles. One may prefer the more Jewish worship style of a Messianic congregation. Another may feel uncomfortable about giving up some control over who his children interact with (i.e., Sunday school teachers, other children). Being accepted at church means giving up some of this freedom for the sake of others. Remember that Messiah promised great rewards to everyone who gives up something for the kingdom (Matthew 19:28–30). The mission is more important than the individual.

Corporate meals are a perfect example. It is hard to go to a potluck and avoid unclean food. A little forethought, though, can make the difficulty disappear. Bring a large helping of a dish that is high in protein and carbohydrates, like cheesy potatoes, and fill up on that. That way, one can still control what he eats, try other things that are obviously clean, and avoid improperly slaughtered meat. One can take the opportunity to make friends and meet people, and talk over dinner. Having this kind of flexibility will go a long way in maintaining a healthy relationship with your church.

Having the heart of a humble servant and showing kindness to others, being affirming and supportive, are all great life skills that are essential to congregational life, whether church or Messianic synagogue.

Another step to blessing the church is to maintain your distinctiveness as a Messianic Gentile. Be different; exemplify the change you wish to see in mainstream Christianity. Are you frustrated that many Christians are not committed enough to discipleship? Be a committed disciple, and make committed disciples. Are you offended at the lack of modesty in many churches? Make it a point to dress modestly and conservatively.

Part of maintaining this distinctiveness will be maintaining a relationship with the broader Messianic community. In time, you may find that the church is receptive to your message, and will become a place where your beliefs are shared and reinforced. But in the meantime, it is important to have the camaraderie and mutual edification that comes from knowing you are not the only one building the Tent. Otherwise, you run the very real risk of losing your distinctiveness as a Messianic Gentile and assimilating into the church as an undifferentiated member. This outcome does nothing to bring much-needed change to the church.

You may be fortunate enough to live near a Messianic synagogue. If so, you may wish to occasionally attend. Even those Messianic synagogues which are more insular may be receptive once they understand what you are trying to do. Messianic Jews desire as much as Messianic Gentiles to see meaningful reform in the church, and will more than likely be happy to support you in what you are doing. Meeting with the local Messianic Jewish rabbi will also give you an opportunity to maintain your direction and passion; it is likely that he will have much to offer in terms of theological and moral support.

Another way to stay connected with the Messianic movement is to attend conferences and special events. Quite a few Messianic Gentiles find themselves refreshed and inspired by our yearly Shavuot conferences or other national gatherings. Events like this help to build and maintain connections with other Messianic believers as well as strengthen one's faith.

First Fruits of Zion also holds regional events to help train and equip Messianic *shlichim*. These annual conferences are a great place to reenergize, recapture a vision for the mission, and refocus one's energy toward the mission of the *shaliach* as outlined in this work. They are also a great place to connect with others who have taken on this mission.

These connections are critical, as the need for interaction, discussion, and training is great. This book is designed to cast a vision for what is necessary and what is possible. However, it is not likely that merely reading a book will be enough to fully prepare one for the mission the Father has set before us. Face-to-face contact, communication, and training with First Fruits of Zion staff and volunteer leaders will help to further flesh out and firm up the ideas portrayed here, and ready one for the mission of taking the message out to the nations. Visit the First Fruits of Zion website at www.ffoz. org to find an event near you.

Another way to be distinct is to hold oneself to the high standard of the Torah. The Messianic Gentile should show people by his actions, by his way of life, how beautiful the Torah is. The mission and message of Yeshua must define his life; if he finds himself in a lukewarm church, he must not settle for anything less than complete commitment on his part. Instead of being frustrated with others' passiveness, he must take the opportunity to play an active role. As Hillel said, "In the place where there are no leaders, strive to be a leader" (*Pirkei Avot* 2:5).

Finally, be positive. Always portray Christianity and Messianic Judaism in a positive light, even though they are not totally in

Show people by your actions, by your way of life, how beautiful the Torah is. The mission and message of Yeshua must define your life; don't settle for anything less than complete commitment on your part.

agreement. Emphasize the good in both faith traditions. As Paul Philip Levertoff wrote, "Christianity is too majestic to live upon the depreciation of rivals."[72] The same is true of Messianic Judaism.

Present the mitzvot as things of beauty, opportunities to connect with God, and not obligations—even if they are obligations. Put them in a positive light and emphasize the things that make them attractive.

Be friendly; smile at people; try to be fun to be around. Use common sense. Enjoy the company of others, and they'll enjoy yours.

DEALING WITH DIFFICULT SITUATIONS

The guidelines above should suffice for the sensitive reader to be able to overcome most obstacles they will encounter as they seek to restore the Jewish Yeshua to the Christian faith. Yet there are a few common problems I want to address as well, as they surface often enough that they warrant specific advice.

The first and probably the most common problem is that church leadership can be resistant to change. This problem is not limited to the Messianic movement, either. Some churches have rejected modern worship music; others eschew any departure from centuries-old liturgies. Both humans and institutions can be resistant to change. The simple fact is that not every single church or Christian will be immediately receptive to their Jewish roots. The best course of action in this situation is to stay in one's church for the church's own sake, even if you find that you cannot effect any change there. Love the church for what it is and love the people for who they are.

One thing to remember in this situation is that change usually comes in small increments. A pastor or congregant might be very receptive to a few key pieces of the Messianic message, but not see how they naturally lead to the others. Just remember that any movement in the right direction is positive. Small, incremental changes are actually better and more sustainable on both the congregational and personal level. They are less stressful and more likely to have staying power than radical, sudden changes.

I have been asked to speak in my church several times. For the first two years I declined. I wanted the people there to be comfortable with me and develop a level of familiarity with me so that when I was given a platform, I would be addressing brethren, friends, and acquaintances instead of strangers. I want people to know where I am coming from and to understand and accept me before I can expect them to understand and accept my message. In this way I hope to provoke small, gradual changes in a way that is gentle and non-confrontational. I believe this attitude has gone a long way in helping me find acceptance at my church.

Another thing to remember is that most people operate best when they are speaking with someone else at their own level. The Messianic Gentile may have a lot of knowledge about the Bible and about Yeshua and Judaism that seems elementary, but for someone who is uninitiated, these concepts are beyond what they are capable of understanding. If the Messianic Gentile finds people totally unreceptive to his message, he may have failed to connect with them on their level. Try talking about something they are interested in, and take the time and effort to build a healthy relationship first.

Another problem many Messianic Gentiles have encountered is anti-Semitism in the church. It is an unfortunate truth that some Christians are anti-Semitic. Anti-Semitism is an irrational hatred of the Jewish people and cannot be countered through argument or debate. It is an indication of a deep spiritual defect and can only be healed through prayer and divine intervention.

Pastors of healthy churches do not want anti-Semites in their congregations, so it is likely that if these tendencies manifest in response to your presence, the Messianic Gentile will not be seen as the problem. Still, sometimes even church leaders can turn out to be anti-Semitic. In this situation it is probably better to find a different church. Not everyone will be receptive to the message of the kingdom.

Similarly, if the Messianic Gentile has done everything he can to support the church and is being forcefully rejected from fellowship and church life because of his beliefs, he should prayerfully consider trying a different church. There are many churches out there

As a Messianic Gentile, you may have a
lot of knowledge about the Bible that
seems elementary, but for someone who
is uninitiated, these concepts are beyond
what they are capable of understanding.

looking for active and knowledgeable people and there is nothing to be gained from staying in a place where one is only causing trouble.

Early childhood education can present another common concern. While teenagers are usually perceptive enough to handle the potential uncomfortable situations, accepting the good and overlooking mistakes, children tend to absorb whatever information they can get. Those with children should take great care to stay informed on the curriculum the church is using, as well as interacting closely with their children and with the teachers in the church. Asking the children to repeat what they have learned is a simple way to give oneself an opportunity to correct any misunderstandings the child may have.

Some Messianic Gentiles might worry that church life will eclipse the distinctive elements of the Messianic worldview in the minds of their children. A suitable analogy can be drawn from the fact that many parents allow their children to watch hours of television, movies, etc., or spend hours on the internet, rather than taking that time to teach and edify their children. Just as it is impossible to expect that an hour at religious services will undo the damage done by a week of irresponsible neglect, it is impossible that an hour of Sunday church will outshine the parents' commitment to taking time daily to lovingly instruct their children.

In Judaism, the center of a child's spiritual education—indeed, the center of spirituality itself—is the home, not the synagogue. Embracing this mindset and wisely using one's time at home with the children to instruct them in the ways of King Messiah will go a long way toward effectively preparing them to critically analyze other messages.

Another area of difficulty involves the observance of Christian holidays. *Some* churches heartily embrace some of the pagan-derived aspects of Easter and Christmas. Understandably, this makes many Messianic Gentiles uncomfortable. The simple solution is not to go during that time of year. People probably won't worry too much about one's absence; in fact, it's quite common for people to be out of town during holidays.

Affirming that you are not judging others will go a
long way toward being accepted by them. Of course,
for this affirmation to be genuine, you must have the
heart of a shaliach, and truly refrain from judging
others for not holding to the same standard you do.

A final area of difficulty is keeping one's level of observance. Some congregants might not immediately understand your reasons for keeping Shabbat, the food laws, the biblical holidays, etc. These misunderstandings can lead to conflict if not handled properly. Disarming the negative feelings people might hold toward the Messianic Gentile's personal observance can be as easy as making it clear that he is not obligating anyone else to the standard he holds, that it is a personal choice he felt led to make. Affirming that one is not judging others will go a long way toward being accepted by them. Of course, for this affirmation to be genuine, one must have the heart of a *shaliach*, and truly refrain from judging others for not holding to the same standard he does.

It is impossible to cover all possible situations here. I hope I have provided the basic tools a Messianic Gentile will need to cultivate a vibrant church life with minimal friction and eventually, if God gives one the opportunity, to bring the message of Christianity's Jewish roots back home to Yeshua's many Gentile followers. It is my hope and prayer that this information will be useful to Messianic Gentiles who seek to advance his kingdom wherever he calls them to minister.

PRIORITIZING THE RIGHT MESSAGE AND RIGHT MISSION

I want to reiterate that the concept of distinction between Jewish and Gentile believers is really essential and integral to the approach I am advocating. It is not possible to bring this message to Christianity any other way. The *shaliach* is doomed to fail if he believes that all Christians are sinning and have thrown off the yoke of God because they do not regard the dietary laws, the sign commandments, and other markers of Jewish identity as things that are required of them. This idea is as offensive to Christians as it is unbiblical. It is counterproductive and has caused untold damage to the movement.

Rather, one should emphasize that his or her observance of mitzvot that the apostles clearly did not lay on Gentiles is a personal choice and not an obligation for all Gentile believers. Even those commandments which Christians are obligated to, but that they have not traditionally understood or applied, should be presented

Please understand that I consider learning about
these commandments to be important for all
believers ... Every commandment of the Torah is
important, and they are all interconnected.

with care, after much deliberation, in the context of a healthy relationship, and in a positive light.

To avoid controversy, many Messianic Gentiles may want to consider making observance of certain optional mitzvot a private matter between them and God. Yeshua teaches that we should perform our acts of righteousness in secret, and not in front of men to be seen by them, or we will receive no reward from our Father who is unseen.

In some cases, a person might have to set aside certain stringencies that he has taken upon himself while he is in the church or dealing with Christians. While it is laudable to want to take on more of God's Torah than one is obligated, in some cases observance of an optional, non-required commandment or custom can actually interfere with observance of a required commandment. For example, if a Messianic Gentile lives with his aging parents, and they are offended at the sight of mezuzot, he should refrain from placing mezuzot on his doorposts in order to honor his father and mother, since as a Gentile he is not required to affix mezuzot.

The apostles chose not to obligate Gentile believers to the commandments of circumcision, Shabbat, festivals, mezuzah, tefillin, tzitzit, or kashrut. These commandments happen to be both optional for Gentiles and controversial for Christians (particularly when practiced by non-Jews). If taking on these commandments or flaunting them in a public manner makes it impossible for someone to take the message of Yeshua's Jewishness into the world and into the church, then those observances are actually hindering one's walk in Torah, not furthering it.

Please understand that I consider learning about these commandments to be important for all believers, and I have no problem with Gentiles honoring God's Sabbaths, holy days, and dietary concerns—in fact, I am encouraged to see all of God's people take an interest in these markedly Jewish practices. Every commandment of the Torah is important, and they are all interconnected. The quiet rest of the Sabbath teaches us to be patient and wait on God. Honoring the Sabbath teaches about the boundaries of holiness, and it brings us into the holiness of the blessed day. So even though some commandments may not be obligatory for Gentile disciples, they are all beautiful and holy, and all of God's children can benefit from them in some way.

PRIORITIZATION AND SENSITIVITY

Even as he seeks to conform his life to God's standard, the Messianic Gentile must be intentional and thoughtful in his application of the Torah's commandments. Two key ideas will help guide him through this process. The first is prioritization. The message of Yeshua's Jewishness must precede the message of obedience to the Torah.

For the average Christian, the first connection point with the beauty and greatness of the Torah should not be external observances like wearing tzitzit. In fact, these external practices may be an initial turn-off, and could bring confusion and identity concerns to an otherwise healthy and receptive congregation. However, when a Christian realizes the Jewishness of Yeshua, he can move from that point to an understanding of the beauty of the Torah.

By prioritizing the more important issues—the core issues—we hope to be able to slowly draw believers in Yeshua toward the Torah and its commandments as they apply to them. When building a house, one starts with the foundation, then erects the wooden beams that form the house's frame, followed by the roof and the walls; only then is he ready to finish the house, to furnish and decorate it. In the same way, Christians must understand the foundational concepts of their faith before they can begin taking on the commandments they are not used to.

Sensitivity is the second core issue. The need to show oneself distinct is as important in settings outside the church as it is in the church. It is important for the Messianic Gentile to show his high regard for Torah and his commitment to its practice, yet do so in such a way that people do not assume he is Jewish. Messianic Gentiles may strongly relate to mitzvot that are incumbent only upon Jews and incorporate aspects of them into their private practice, but they must respect the distinct relationship of the Jewish people to God, Israel, and Torah without acting or appearing in public or, especially, in Jewish or Messianic Jewish settings in a way that gives onlookers the impression that they are Jewish.

Since the well-grounded Messianic Gentile is comfortable with his identity and understands which mitzvot are obligatory for Jews but are optional for him, he can avoid such confusion by not wearing ceremonial Jewish apparel like tzitzit, tallit, and tefillin in public, and especially in Jewish and Messianic Jewish settings. (It is, however, appropriate for all men, both Jews and Gentiles, to wear a kippah when inside a synagogue.) In this way he can be sensitive to the concerns of Messianic Jews, and show them that Messianic Gentiles can love the Torah profoundly and pervasively while being deeply respectful of Jewish identity and the obligations of Torah that are incumbent upon Jews.

We have attempted to address these matters in a sensitive manner in our *Mayim Chayim* (living water) series of books which deals with the individual commandments in a detailed manner. Drawing from our most recent edition, on tzitzit, Toby Janicki states:

> A Gentile believer who wears a *tallit katan* throughout the day would be well served to tuck in his tzitzit so they are out of sight and not attracting attention. It also might be best to reserve the use of a *tallit gadol* for the privacy of his personal prayer time. As we have stated, tzitzit are a visible sign to both the world and other Jews that one is Jewish (and for that matter practicing Orthodox Judaism). Wearing them visibly can be like false advertising, and it communicates disrespect for the Jewish people. The Jewish community generally perceives Gentiles wearing tzitzit or praying with a *tallit gadol* in public as offensive. It looks like deception to Jews, and to non-Jewish believers, it looks something like kids playing cowboy—dressing up Jewish. Additionally when Gentiles wear visible tzitzit and do things that violate Orthodox tradition it can be a stumbling block ... While I do not want to be dogmatic, non-Jews who take up this mitzvah should consider keeping its observance private, tucking their tzitzit in, and refraining from wearing a *tallit gadol* during public services.

By following the path of steady, meticulous, strategic change, rather than pushing people to accept an avalanche of new things all at once, I hope to see multitudes of believers embrace the Torah as it applies to them—both Jews and Gentiles. If the Torah is presented correctly, with the foundation laid first, our message has great potential to be accepted, and to change the lives of millions.

JARS OF CLAY

Paul wrote (2 Corinthians 4:5–12):

> For what we proclaim is not ourselves, but Jesus Christ as Lord, with ourselves as your servants for Jesus' sake. For God, who said, "Let light shine out of darkness," has shone in our hearts to give the light of the knowledge of the glory of God in the face of Jesus Christ. But we have this treasure in jars of clay, to show that the surpassing power belongs to God and not to us. We are afflicted in every way, but not crushed; perplexed, but not driven to despair; persecuted, but not forsaken; struck down, but not destroyed; always carrying in the body the death of Jesus, so that the life of Jesus may also be manifested in our bodies. For we who live are always being given over to death for Jesus' sake, so that the life of Jesus also may be manifested in our mortal flesh. So death is at work in us, but life in you.

Paul's attitude is desperately important for the *shaliach* to adopt. Though the Messianic Gentile may find it incredibly difficult to negotiate the tension between his faith and practice and that of his brothers and sisters in mainstream Christianity, he must continue to work steadily for the sake of Yeshua the Messiah.

It may be that, like Paul, the *shaliach* will have to make sacrifices to communicate the Father's message in a way that people will accept. He may have to change his appearance or mannerisms in order to more successfully connect with others. He may, even then, be persecuted for being different. But in this, he must remember that he is not his own; he is merely a receptacle for something bigger and more important than himself.

Let us rejoice in the high calling and mission that we have been given. Let us embody the message of Yeshua, the message of repentance and faithfulness. For the benefit of others, of Christianity, of the entire world, the *shaliach* sacrifices his own ambitions and desires. For this, the reward is great.

"The surpassing power belongs to God, and not to us." The spirit of God will continue to direct and guide the Messianic Gentile who takes on the mission of communicating his faith to others. Depend on God, pray steadfastly, and realize that you are not alone, that you are part of something bigger, something incredible. In this flood of information, don't lose sight of the fact that God is moving, and that we are only caught up in his movement.

Strategic Mission

The mission of the
Messianic Gentile, broken
down into simple, easy steps.

This book outlines a vast mission and vision. At first it can seem overwhelming both in the scope it entails and in the sacrifice it requires. However, we believe it is possible for even one person or one family to make a difference in their church and in their community. To this end, I have included a strategic mission, designed to aid and give concrete direction to a person or group of people who have been called to take on this mission.

Every strategic mission begins with a vision. This vision is the all-encompassing, seemingly impossible, world-changing goal toward which we set our eyes as we go about our day-to-day business. The strategic mission and everything else it entails are born out of the vision and exist solely for the fulfillment of the vision.

◊ Vision: *To bring the church back to its foundations, eliminate supersessionism, establish a Jewish understanding of faith in Yeshua, and bring the church into solidarity with Israel.*

The mission is the day-to-day business of the *shaliach*. It represents what he hopes to accomplish on a daily basis as he works slowly toward the realization of the vision.

◊ Mission: *To engage traditional Christians in a positive and affirming manner and draw them, one person at a time, to a deeper knowledge of their own faith and its Jewish roots.*

REALITY ASSESSMENT

Every vision requires change. Healthy, positive change is the action of moving something from where it is to where it should be. One must understand where and what something currently is before trying to move or alter it. Through extensive collaboration with a national network of volunteers, we have come up with four basic realities, statements that define where the church is now and that represent the difficulty inherent in undertaking this mission.

◊ First, the church does not want what we have. Churches have literally hundreds of thousands of resources at their disposal, disseminated by hundreds of publishing companies. While there may be a desire for change, most churches have no reason to believe that the solution lies outside mainstream Christianity. Rather, if a church realizes that it has problems, it is more likely to look to popular Christian programming for solutions, believing that the fault lies in its application of Christian doctrine to its situation, and not in a fundamental misreading of Scripture. The bottom line is that churches think they are correct, that they should be changing others, not that they need to be corrected or changed. That is an absolutely fundamental mindset in most Christian circles (though there are exceptions).

◊ Second, many Christians suffer from complacency. The popular Christian gospel message is a simple intellectual assent to statements of doctrine. It has no mechanism for change; change is assumed to happen on its own as a work of the Holy Spirit (codified as "sanctification" in systematic theology). This theological mindset has led many Christians to take a passive approach to social and moral problems both in society and in the church, as well as to their own spiritual growth and maturity. There are exceptions, people who have gone to great lengths to bring change in these areas, but this is not the case for most Christians.

◊   Third, much of Christian leadership is addicted to the status quo. Changing a formula that is thought to be divinely ordained is a scary proposition. Especially in more ancient denominations, leaders have to be very careful about any deviation from established dogma. By and large, most Christian leaders do not have the courage to risk taking a doctrinal stand that runs contrary to that of their denomination. Even in churches that have nothing to lose in this area, many are unwilling to risk changing a formula that works in their church, out of fear of offending or isolating some of their congregants.

◊   Fourth, people who wish to effect change in churches have to make great sacrifices. If they are in positions of leadership, especially paid positions, they may be risking their ministry and their livelihood; but even those not in positions of authority have sacrifices to make. It is difficult to be different. It might be hard to build deep friendships. There may be people who want to draw the dissenting voice into never-

ending theological arguments and attempt to
discredit them. There may be personal attacks
and rivalries. But even when all is peaceful, it
is still not easy to worship in a way to which
someone is not accustomed or fully agrees with.
To a Messianic Gentile this adjustment can be
uncomfortable and even painful.

MISSION OBJECTIVES

The four priority issues which Messianic Gentiles should focus on
in their efforts to accomplish the mission are the same as the four
pillars mentioned in the book: the Jewishness of Yeshua, God's
continued covenantal relationship with Israel, the continuing relevance and binding authority of the Torah, and the gospel of the
kingdom of heaven.

These four issues together represent the great failure of Christianity to adhere to its roots as a sect of Judaism. The fact that they
were lost is a testament to the church's desire to sever itself from her
mother faith, Second Temple Judaism, and her sister faith, modern
Judaism. Intertwined with this schism is the idea that the church
constitutes the only people of God, the only people who have an outstanding covenant with God, and the only people who will be saved.
This is the essence of supersessionism and of its many offshoots.

Correcting these four errors is foundational to the accomplishment of the mission. The rest of what is lacking in Christianity can
be addressed from a solidly grounded foundation in which the church
realizes the Jewishness of her Messiah, her everlasting bond with
God's covenant people Israel, her obligation to God as directed in
the Torah as it was mediated and interpreted by the apostles, and
her obligation to change the world via an active, living gospel.

GOALS

At this stage of the strategic mission, concrete goals are set. These goals are measurable and attainable. They represent real, meaningful steps toward the accomplishment of the mission and the realization of the vision.

◊ The first goal of this mission is for Messianic Gentiles to become a noble presence in Christian churches. They must be respectful and deferential so that their presence is not seen as a threat or a nuisance. They must begin to show Christianity that the Messianic movement is not its enemy, but rather, that Messianic Gentiles are an important, supportive, and helpful part of the church.

◊ The second goal is for Messianic Gentiles to begin opening dialogue concerning the four great historical errors of the Christian church. It is important to be able to start a discussion on these topics without becoming emotionally charged or fostering a climate of negativity. It may take years before the church is ready and the time is appropriate to begin this basic level of dialogue.

◊ The third goal is for Messianic Gentiles to win respect for themselves and their views. The church and its leadership must grow to view the Messianic movement and its theology in a positive light. This respect is mutual; the

Messianic Gentile must also respect and value
traditional Christianity.

◊ The fourth goal is for Messianic Gentiles to
become a trusted and valued component of the
church. At this point, Messianic Gentiles will be
relied on to provide accurate information about
Christianity's origins and its Jewish roots. This
information will begin to impact the church and
its theology.

VALUES OF A SHALIACH

The values of a *shaliach* are the character traits that people who
desire to implement the plan must possess. These values are critical
to the success of the mission and help to embody and represent the
vision in a real sense on a small scale. Without holding these values,
it will be difficult or impossible to undertake the mission without
experiencing disillusion and burnout.

In this book I have referred to the type of person who is suited
for the mission outlined in this strategic mission as a *shaliach*, a "sent
one." The term *shaliach* sums up and epitomizes a certain value set
that is vital to accomplishing the mission. These values all have to
do with how one person relates to another, as the duty of a *shaliach*
is to take the message to others with a view toward its acceptance,
and for the message to be accepted, the messenger must be as well.

◊ A *shaliach* must embrace the idea that all of
God's people are legitimate children. They are
justified—declared righteous, declared to be
good. This fundamental goodness derives from
the very righteousness of Christ himself; to

deny it is to deny the power of Christ to justify. Accepting God's people as brothers and sisters in spite of their faults is a necessary consequence of this justification.

◊ A *shaliach* must be honest, genuine, and sincere. If he thinks he is going undercover into the church like a secret agent, it will end in disaster. This is completely the wrong approach. A *shaliach* builds real relationships with no ulterior motive, and sincerely desires to see people grow closer to Yeshua. He is graceful and never pushes people to accept a concept or practice they are not willing to accept. He continues to love and value people for who they are regardless of how they react to his message.

◊ A *shaliach* must present his message confidently yet humbly, with grace and integrity. He must keep the essence of the message intact without compromising anything; yet his delivery must be full of grace and mercy. He must hope to bring change, yet be humble and realistic about what he, as just one person, can do. In the same vein, the *shaliach* must be a zealot for Messiah and for the message Messiah has for his people; yet in regard to himself, he must remember that he is only a vessel, and as Abraham our father said of himself, "only dust and ashes" (Genesis 18:27).

◊ A *shaliach* must conform his own life to the message he delivers. He is reaching the church with the message that the Torah is relevant, that it informs the Gentile believer's obligation to God; he had better live out these obligations himself. Many Christians could benefit greatly from the high ethical standard which is represented in Jewish *mussar* literature; the *shaliach* should personify this standard and live a life that is beyond reproach.

◊ A *shaliach* must be willing to sacrifice for the kingdom, for the propagation of the message of Messiah to the world. For Chabad *shlichim*, this usually involves at the very least moving to a new location, leaving behind the comfortable community in which everyone shares the same values, living on a shoestring budget, dedicating all of their spare time to the mission, making phone calls, house calls, building relationships, being vulnerable. It is difficult to imagine that Christ would expect any less of his *shlichim*.

◊ A *shaliach* must be patient and stoic, able to weather long periods of spiritual drought in anticipation of the rain and harvest that is coming. It may take months or years to lay the groundwork for a particular mission.

TOUCH-POINTS

Godly wisdom must govern the actions of a true *shaliach*. A *shaliach* must be sensitive to the Spirit's prompting on what to teach and when, on when to be silent and when to speak and remember at all times this principle, "All my days have I grown up among the wise and I have not found anything better for a man than silence. Studying Torah is not the most important thing rather fulfilling it. Whoever multiplies words causes sin" (*Pirkei Avot* 1:17).

When the opportunity to share does present itself, priorities must be set, the audience must be considered, and the right message delivered. Following is a list of "touch-points" developed by my friend Aaron Hopper who is engaged in this mission. Aaron says, "from a practical point of view, these are some of the topics on which I have taught in multiple churches that generally produce a very positive response with little offense or argument. As such, they seem to me to be good 'touch-points' for the church to experience the Jewishness of our faith and Messiah."

◊ *There is grace in the Torah.* Many Christians think grace is a topic exclusively found in the New Testament. I have taught on *chesed* from the Torah and demonstrated how stories and events display God's *chesed*.

◊ *"Old Testament" saints were saved by faith, not the blood of bulls and goats.* Many believers think that Old Testament saints were saved by the sacrifices. Teaching especially from Hebrews, I explain how salvation has always come through faith, and that the sacrifices were not a different method of salvation, but rather a living out of faith—faith in action. This shows Christians the continuity between Torah and New Testament and how the New Testament amplifies and explains Torah. It can also lead into the fuller meaning of faith expressed in obedience to God's commands.

◊ *The festivals are valuable for believers.* I explain the purpose and rich imagery behind the festivals and show that Yeshua observed them. Christians are usually very receptive to studies on the festivals.

◊ *The "10 commandments" cannot be ripped from context.* I teach that there is no moral, civil, ceremonial distinction in God's Torah and challenge believers on their assumptions about morality.

◊ *The purpose of the Torah and its continuing value.* It is very easy and beneficial to teach about the purposes for which God gave Torah and show why it is still valuable to believers. This can be done in a way that does not offend or make anyone feel as if they must observe it. They can be left to draw their own conclusions.

◊ *The church's relationship to Israel.* Modern evangelicals tend to be pro-Israel, but they rarely can articulate why or what the relationship of the church to Israel is, biblically speaking.

◊ *Any reference or allusion to an Old Testament event or passage.* Anytime the New Testament quotes or refers to an Old Testament event, I take the class to that passage or event and provide whatever context to it that I am able to provide.

◊ *The Jewishness of early believers and worship.* Few Christians have studied early church history, and they have usually not considered how many early believers were Jewish or what a close relationship the early church had with the synagogues.

◊ *The influence of the synagogue system on the church.* Believers are surprised to see the parallels between synagogue worship and church worship.

◊ *Paul's Jewishness and rabbinic style of expression.* There are frequent opportunities for me when teaching on epistles to highlight Paul's Jewish thinking. For example, Paul's use of *kal v'chomer* (simple to complex) is plentiful.

◊ *The robust nature of salvation and the gospel.* Salvation and the gospel are so much more majestic than "believe in facts and go to heaven." I teach heavily on the bodily resurrection, the New Jerusalem, the restoration of heaven and earth, etc. I particularly enjoyed N.T. Wright's book, *Surprised by Hope*, which makes a similar argument.

◊ *Add context whenever possible.* Anytime possible, even when listening and not teaching, I attempt to remind Christians of the importance of context. I love to amplify Jesus' parables with the Jewish context, and I have used Daniel Lancaster's short audio clip on the "Macaroni Principle" dozens of times. Christians always want to know where I got that clip—it is eye opening, friendly, and relatable.

THE MISSION FIELD

A strategic mission must include a target demographic, a people group that is most likely to respond to the message. There are some types of churches that will be more amenable than others to the message of Yeshua's Jewishness. We stated above that older denominations, such as Catholic, Orthodox, and Reformed, are more resistant to change due to their more established governmental systems and more developed systematic theology. This problem is less marked in Evangelical churches, Baptist denominations, and their offshoots, as individual churches in these circles are encouraged, empowered, and expected to develop their own polity and doctrine, within guidelines that are generally broader than those developed by other denominations. Independent churches, Bible churches, and charismatic churches tend to be even looser, yet many have resilient doctrinal systems of their own.

The best approach is to remain in or engage a church that one is familiar with or a church in a denomination that one is familiar with, whether liturgical or charismatic, traditional or contemporary, Reformed or Baptist, etc. The more familiarity the *shaliach* has with the way the church operates currently, the better position he will be in to offer loving, healthy correction if the opportunity arises.

Conclusion

Rebuild the Tent,
Honor the Messiah,
Change the Church.

n this book, I have tried to communicate a vision for the restoration of the apostle's initial, formative vision for Christianity. My desire is to see the Tent of David restored, to see Gentiles from all nations come alongside the Messianic Jewish movement and recognize Yeshua as the Jewish Messiah and King of the Jews, to see Messianic Gentiles engage their churches with the richness and depth they have gleaned from their study of Christianity's Jewish roots.

For twenty years, my team and I at First Fruits of Zion have labored to make this vision a reality. In that time, we have seen myriads of believers come to an understanding of Yeshua's Jewishness, leave behind supersessionism, and begin taking their obligations as believers seriously. They have experienced a great renewal in their walk with the Lord, and their spiritual journey has been rejuvenated. Yet out of all those Messianic Gentiles, comparatively few have been able to make significant headway in reaching the church with their message.

Yet there have been many success stories as well. I know of one Messianic Gentile who, after unsuccessfully trying to start a house church, decided to swallow his pride and join a local church. He supported the mission and vision of the church and affirmed what he held in common with them. He began taking courses at a seminary in order to be able to engage Christianity on its own terms.

Today he is an associate pastor. He has influenced five other pastors in the immediate area to shift their theology toward a post-supersessionist mindset. He is part of his denomination's governing structure, helping to oversee hundreds of churches in his region. Yet in all this, he has never had to compromise his standards.

At another church in the same state, there is a thriving Torah Club small group with as many members as a small church. At some point, an elderly Messianic Gentile lady had to decide to stay in that church and make a difference there, and it has paid off handsomely. She now has all six of our Torah Clubs used in her church with hundreds in attendance. She is making a big difference.

I know of pastors that have respected the desire of some members of their church body to study the Torah on Sabbath and encouraged them to host Sabbath study groups in the church's facility. Those groups now have become significant aspects of the church's discipleship programs.

Consider the multiplicative influence of these people alone. How many people will eventually be affected by their efforts, as people continue to share what they have learned with others? The sacrifices they have made and the obstacles they have overcome seem insignificant in comparison to the influence they have been able to have in the church—and these are just several of many who have taken the same path.

I have had numerous people from my church come to my home for Sabbath meals. Each time the conversation has naturally flowed to the beauty and need for the Sabbath in today's world. Through their experiences in my home, they have now considered the Sabbath as something relevant and healthy as opposed to something oppressive and obsolete.

The Tent of David can absolutely be restored. Messianic Gentiles can change the church, and with it, the world. I believe this is God's plan. All that remains is for more people who have already been impacted by the Jewish Yeshua to take his message into the church and for the church to bring it to the nations.

Some Messianic Gentiles may be reluctant to take on this mission because they feel that their place is within greater Judaism and among the Jewish people. After decades of serving in this movement, I want to state emphatically that *Judaism does not need or want*

Gentiles taking on Jewish identity or becoming Jewish. Gentiles coming to synagogues and trying to integrate with the Jewish community often causes more harm than good. Their presence provokes fears of assimilation and concerns about losing the Jewish people's unique identity. It provokes anger to see Gentiles take on uniquely Jewish customs. It is perceived as misguided at best, and arrogant and supersessionist at worst. I have seen it again and again. Gentiles who take this route are often setting themselves up for disappointment.

I understand that Gentiles going to synagogue is the apostolic model. In fact, it was the only option for Messianic Gentiles in the apostolic period. First Fruits of Zion has been teaching this for decades. Perhaps at some point in the future, the hundreds of years of hate and misunderstanding will have been forgiven and forgotten, and synagogue attendance will again be a viable option. But for this scenario to exist, Messianic Gentiles must first change the church, and Messianic Jews must reconnect with Judaism.

Until that time, Judaism does not need Gentiles coming to synagogue. What Judaism really needs is *billions of friends.* Judaism needs the uncountable numbers of Christians around the world to stand up for the plight of the Jewish people and plead their cause to the nations. Israel needs Christians to be her advocate in the tension-filled Middle East. The Jews need Christians to help *prevent another Holocaust, not facilitate one by encouraging assimilation and conformity—by continuing to deprecate the value of being Jewish and the covenant responsibilities of the Jewish people.*

As I write this, the day after *Yom HaShoah* (Holocaust Remembrance Day in Israel), Jewish bloggers are lamenting the loss of millions of American Jews over the past few decades—not through death, but through assimilation. This assimilation, the "American Holocaust," is facilitated by a society that sees Jewishness as irrelevant, a society built on Christian values that were propagated by a church that also saw Jewishness as irrelevant.

The burden for this tragedy, for the secular anti-Semitism which led to the Holocaust, and for a large portion of Jewish animosity toward Christianity (via the Crusades, the Inquisition, and other atrocities) is properly laid at the feet of the church. I stated above that the church is good, and it is. Yet often, "good is the enemy of great."[73] Christianity is at its weakest when it assumes that having an intellectual belief in Yeshua is enough, that it is good enough to profess the name of Christ without taking action to repair the world. The complacence this mindset cultivates has caused millions of Christians to abandon their mission.

Judaism does not need Gentiles coming to synagogue.
What Judaism really needs is billions of friends to
help prevent another Holocaust, not facilitate one
by encouraging assimilation and conformity.

Christianity is good, but it could be great. It could fulfill its prophetic role by coming alongside Israel and supporting the Jewish people in their mission to reflect God to the world, to manifest holiness, justice, and the character of God to the nations, to restore the Tent of David. Messianic Gentiles are waking up to this reality all over the globe.

The time is ripe, however, to take this mission into the church, to multiply *shlichim*, to renew and restore Christianity with a sense of its original mission, purpose, and relationship to the Jewish people. Never have there been more resources to facilitate this mission. Never have there been more Christians willing to accept the Jewish Yeshua. Never has the scholarly landscape been so open to a Torah-observant, fully Jewish Yeshua and Paul. Never has the church so clearly realized that something is missing, that something is wrong, that something needs to change.

If you are a Messianic Gentile, you have a concrete mission and calling as part of the Gentile body of Messiah. In all probability, your encounter with the Jewish Yeshua and the Torah have clarified and crystallized that calling in your own life. I urge you to consider taking the Jewish Yeshua with you into your church, so that other Christians can begin to get a sense of that calling in their own lives.

In order for the apostles' original vision for the restored Tent of David to become a reality, Christians absolutely must understand the foundations of their faith. They must understand that their Messiah, Yeshua the Messiah, is a Jew, the prophesied King Messiah, and still today the King of the Jews. They must understand their relationship with Israel, that God's calling of the descendants of Jacob is irrevocable and permanent, and that Christians are partners along with the Jewish people in an economy of mutual blessing. They must understand that the apostles framed the obligations of the Gentile believer using the Torah and traditional Jewish values and that these obligations need to be taken seriously. They must rediscover their own gospel message and the power it has to change the world.

The mission of the Messianic Gentile is to bear witness to these four concepts; the greatest opportunity to do this is to graciously engage the church. It won't be easy. It requires sacrifice, diligence, and patience. The Messianic Gentile may struggle; he may encounter failure. He may, like our Master, have to endure heartbreak and persecution for a time. But the mission is great, and the reward is great.

Against all odds, Christianity went from a band of twelve to the world's largest religion. Though there may be comparatively few Messianic Gentiles today, I believe the Father will choose to bless and empower their efforts to reach the church and the world with the message of King Messiah, the King of the Jews, Yeshua the Messiah.

But it depends on you. Will you accept the mission? Will you brave the danger to earn the reward? Will you dedicate your life to something bigger than yourself? Will you do your part to restore the Tent of David?

> The day is short, the task is abundant, the laborers are lazy, the wage is great, and the Master of the house is insistent. (*Pirkei Avot* 2:20)

Become a *shaliach* for *Mashiach*.

What Makes Churches Different

Seek first to understand in order to
be understood. Learn why people
believe what they believe.

Assumption is the foundation of all poor communication. One of the biggest barriers to all interfaith (or intrafaith—between two people who share the same faith) communication is the assumption that when two people use the same word, they must be talking about the same thing. For example, the definitions to words like "faith," "redemption," "repentance," and "sin" might seem obvious to both Jews and Christians. However, these words have different—sometimes vastly different—meanings within the two respective faiths.

In light of this fact, in this appendix we will explore what makes the various denominations of Christianity different from each other and what their respective core beliefs are. We will discuss the lenses through which they tend to read the Bible and the best ways to approach someone of any given Christian background with the message of Yeshua the Jewish Messiah.

The first thing to consider is that, for the most part, every institutional church believes that it is in direct continuity with the New Testament church and with the apostles themselves. Nearly every church that has a timeline of church history will portray itself as a straight line from the beginning of the apostolic church until the end of time; other churches inevitably drift off the central line into apostasy. Alternately, the "true" church has reformed or been restored to the original, pristine vision of the apostles, while all other denominations stubbornly persist in error.

This need to be right, to affirm one's own correctness and immunity from error, is a hallmark of churches which rely on dogmatic beliefs to differentiate between insiders and outsiders. Due to the reliance on dogma, churches often become insular and it becomes difficult for them to consider a different point of view. Alternative theologies are stigmatized not just as being incorrect, but as being heretical. Many Christians are so sensitized to differences in dogma that anything which appears even slightly foreign will immediately be rejected.

The *shaliach* will inevitably come up against this attitude in the church. Because of this, it is important for him to know where the beliefs he is dealing with have come from, how to use terminology that the church he is in will recognize, and where to find a "handle" or connection point from which to begin communicating to people in the church in which he has been called to witness.

Disagreement is usually mitigated to discussion when one understands the other's position and is able to articulate it. The goal of this section is to give you a sense of variances, core beliefs, and values of several denominations so that you will be able to balance your views with an understanding of theirs. For years I have been guided by the mantra, "Seek first to understand in order to be understood." Assumption and ignorance will make the role of a *shaliach* difficult and will produce little fruit.

BAPTIST, ANABAPTIST, BIBLE, AND NON-DENOMINATIONAL CHURCHES

Baptist churches have their roots in the Anabaptist movement of the sixteenth century. As Luther's reforms began to inspire people to take a closer look at Christian faith and practice, a group of radical believers, all of whom had been baptized as infants in the Roman Catholic Church, began to question the legitimacy of their baptisms. Not being able to find a precedent for infant baptism in the New Testament, these Anabaptists—rebaptizers—began to immerse each other in an attempt to return to a Biblical model of baptism.

The fundamental driving force behind the Anabaptist movement and all of its subsequent offshoots is the desire to totally reform

Christianity to be faithful to its scriptural roots. The concept of tradition is almost totally eschewed, even further than in Reformed churches. If justification for a certain practice or doctrine cannot be found in the Bible, it is theoretically free to be called into question.

Baptist churches, at least partly because of what they perceived to be the abuses of power in the Catholic and early Reformed churches, have traditionally resisted centralized denominational structures. A Baptist denomination generally gives its churches a lot of leeway to make their own decisions; as much as it can be, authority is decentralized. The local church owns the land and the buildings, in contrast to many older denominations in which the denominational superstructure owns the church's property. Baptist churches also tend to be congregational, rather than having elders, bishops, or presbyters make decisions for the entire church.

Many Baptist churches have no denominational affiliation; they are sometimes called "Independent," but often have no specific indicator. Other types of churches, such as Bible churches and many (if not most) nondenominational churches with no obvious affiliation in their title, are essentially Baptist or have strong roots in the Baptist tradition. The primary identifiers for a Baptist (or similar) church are the practice of adult baptism by immersion and congregational leadership. Most traditional Baptists also reject the Charismatic Renewal and believe that the so-called "sign" gifts of the Holy Spirit are not active today.

Modern Baptist churches are generally split along the lines of the Fundamentalist-Modernist controversy of the early twentieth century. Southern Baptist and Independent Baptist churches tend to be Fundamentalist; they reject modern scientific theories as to the age of the universe, the evolution of species, and higher criticism of the Bible. Many other Baptist denominations are Modernist; they have embraced these modern ideas to some extent or another. This controversy has left many Fundamentalist churches with a sense of battle-weariness; they may have difficulty accepting new ideas as they feel they have already fought off the heresies of the modern age and are the only Baptists who remain true to the Scriptures.

Similarly, Fundamentalist Baptists tend to resist ecumenism; there is a strong current of resistance in these circles to Reformed (Calvinist) and Roman Catholic doctrine, and any thought of compromise with other belief systems (including Judaism) is seen as a step in the wrong direction.

Baptist churches have nevertheless been the richest source of Messianic Gentiles for several reasons. First, Baptist churches have a history of rejecting tradition in favor of the scriptural witness (as they perceive it). This is not so different from the path to becoming a Messianic Gentile, as the Messianic faith has gone even further than the Baptist in questioning Christian dogma and reinterpreting the New Testament in its original context.

Second, Baptist churches emphasize the individual, personal study of Scripture. As a result, many Baptists have read and studied the Old Testament and have legitimate questions about its interpretation.

Third, Baptist churches have a high degree of freedom to choose how to practice and teach on a local level. Not being forced into a certain mold by their denomination, they may have an easier time integrating a more Messianic perspective into Bible studies and sermons without having to deal with retribution from a higher church authority.

The *shaliach* can help the Baptist get back in touch with his own foundational principles by showing him (gently, in the context of a relationship, as this book describes) how the Messianic faith is genuine and Biblically based, and represents a complete return to a New Testament faith that does not depend on later traditions.

METHODIST CHURCHES

The Methodist Church was founded by John Wesley and several other men in the eighteenth century. These men were unhappy with the state of Anglicanism and sought to bring reform. Their name derives from the methodical approach they took to spiritual life, reflecting their desire to reach a high degree of holiness.

Methodism, due to its roots in the Anglican Church, is not congregational as the Baptist churches are. Instead, important decisions are made by bishops, who lead the churches in their region. Pastors are appointed rather than elected, and are accountable to denominational leadership.

Methodism today is divided. Like several of the old Reformed denominations, the United Methodist Church focuses more on social issues than some of the more conservative denominations. United Methodists have taken a more liberal approach to creation science as well, having generally come down on the Modernist side of the Fundamentalist-Modernist controversy. Furthermore, there is a strong movement within United Methodism to allow for the acceptance of homosexual activity, though as of this writing, the denominational leadership still does not allow it.

The Free Methodist Church and the various other Wesleyan denominations are generally more conservative. Yet many of these churches are also finding it difficult to retain the original focus of Methodism—personal holiness—as they have been swept up in the Evangelical movement, which has tended to homogenize Baptist and Free Methodist churches, among many others, around the idea of the simple gospel message.

A Methodist church can be distinguished from churches of other denominations by the use of the term "Methodist" or "Wesleyan" in its name, a top-down leadership structure, infant baptism, and usually, strong Arminian theology and a resistance to reformed Calvinism.

The *shaliach* can help the practicing Methodist return to his own foundational principles by emphasizing the importance of holiness and how the Torah is instrumental in defining exactly what holiness is. The "methodical" practices inherent to the Messianic faith may appeal to Methodists who are interested in reconnecting with that aspect of their own faith. In any case, even a return to the devout and serious practice of the early Methodists would be a great step, for many Methodists, toward the Torah and toward holiness.

ANCIENT LITURGICAL CHURCHES

The Roman Catholic Church is the largest denomination of Christianity. It predates the Reformed, Baptist, and Methodist churches and all other Protestant denominations. It is the western branch of what used to be a unified, nearly monolithic expression of Christianity that extended across the remnants of the Roman Empire and traced its ancestry directly back to the early church fathers. The eastern branch broke off in the eleventh century and is now the Eastern Orthodox Church, the second largest denomination of Christianity.

The two halves remain similar in many ways. They both retain an ancient liturgical form of worship and their respective theologies often emphasize the same concepts. At least compared to the modern non-denominational church, they appear quite similar. This section will emphasize the Catholic Church as, for geographical and statistical reasons, it is currently more likely that the average Messianic Gentile will encounter Catholicism than Orthodoxy.

The Catholic and Orthodox churches are decidedly different from the Protestant denominations. Catholicism emphasizes the dispensation of God's grace through sacraments, whereas Protestants believe that grace is dispensed freely with no cooperation from the believer. Orthodox Christians, like Catholics, emphasize the very real connection with God which occurs through the "Sacred Mysteries," their name for the practices called "sacraments" in the Catholic Church.

Catholic children are baptized; this is thought to be the first sacrament, or dispensation of sanctifying grace. Later on, the child will have his first confession, followed by his first Eucharist. Later still, the child is confirmed and becomes an adult. Many Catholics will either marry or take holy orders, becoming priests. Finally, the very sick are anointed. For the dying, this anointing is one of several sacraments that make up the "last rites." These seven sacraments are mirrored in the Mysteries of the Orthodox Church and are taken just as seriously.

The repeated administration of the Eucharist, "the source and summit of the Christian life,"[74] both represents and actually effects a mystical union with Christ, as the bread and wine literally become Christ's body and blood. Continual participation in the Eucharist and other sacraments serves to suppress the natural instinct of man and help him to turn his heart back toward God. The liturgy of the Mass (in Orthodoxy, the "Divine Liturgy"), which is ideally repeated daily, is a constant reminder of Christ and a constant call to holy living.

More than in other denominations, suffering is an important concept in Catholicism. Earth is not heaven; it is not a place of joy, but a place of suffering. As Catholics suffer, they identify with the suffering of Christ, as formally represented in the Stations of the

Cross. Meditation on the suffering of Christ, as pictured in the ubiquitous crucifix, helps the Catholic to be grateful, to dedicate his life to God, and to live his life for others.

The Catholic Church is well known for its hierarchical structure. The Pope is the leader of the church; he is elected by a specially appointed, senior group of bishops called cardinals. Bishops, the main administrative unit of the Catholic Church, oversee dioceses. Each diocese is divided into parishes, each of which is administered by a priest. The priest administers the sacraments to Catholics in his parish.

Orthodox churches, while organized similarly, do not look to one primary leader; rather, they are a large group of self-governing regional churches, not governed by a single bishop or patriarch. While the Patriarch of Constantinople is senior, he is "first among equals" and does not have ecclesiastical power over the leaders of other Orthodox churches.

Catholics and Protestants have several historic disputes. Catholics are often condemned for being exclusivist, for teaching that only Catholics go to heaven. However, most Catholics today believe that all believers go to heaven; Catholics are privileged to have the fullness of truth, but do not necessarily receive more grace just for being Catholic.

Catholics also do not believe in works-based salvation, as Protestants have historically accused them. However, they do believe that works are a necessary accompaniment to faith (and not merely its natural consequence, as Protestants teach); without good works one does not inherit eternal life. One cannot profess to believe and simultaneously neglect to do good.

A further difference: Protestants believe that only the Scriptures are authoritative. Catholics, on the other hand, have an authoritative body of tradition (the Magisterium) stretching back to the days of the early church fathers.

The Catholic Church is often criticized for other reasons; it is plagued by the violent legacy of the medieval church, as well as by modern-day scandals. However, the devout Catholic is not violent or lascivious. Catholics are concerned with living a life of holiness, being one with Christ, and helping other people.

As traditional as the Catholic Church is, it has been remarkably progressive in repudiating anti-Semitism. The papal declaration *Nostra Aetate* (October 28, 1965) acknowledged the church's roots in Judaism and decried persecution of any kind, and specifically that directed at the Jewish people. It also affirmed that the Jewish people had not been rejected or cursed by God. Catholics continue to be pioneers in Jewish-Christian dialogue. Even more, the Association of Hebrew Catholics (AHC) seeks to protect and preserve the Jewish identity of Catholics of Jewish origin.

The *shaliach* can help the Catholic connect to his own foundational principles by reinforcing the ideas of holiness, devotion, and continual sanctification through good works, all of which are important in both Messianic Judaism and in the Catholic faith. The *shaliach* can also gradually help Catholics internalize the Catholic Church's shift in teaching on the Jews since the Second Vatican Council, which produced *Nostra Aetate*. Encouraging and affirming this progress, and helping the average Catholic to understand its implications, is the next step forward. One can also support the work of the AHC in helping Catholic Jews to preserve their identity and calling.

The *shaliach* can also affirm the value of tradition, and slowly introduce the idea that the apostles would have been familiar with an even older stream of tradition, the Jewish oral tradition. However, as Catholicism and Orthodoxy are comparatively monolithic, highly organized, and dogmatic religions, one should be especially careful not to press their adherents to change their theology or practice. Rather, being kind, affirmative, and gentle, the *shaliach* should introduce people to new concepts without projecting his own expectations onto them.

TRADITIONAL PROTESTANT CHURCHES

Presbyterian, Lutheran, and Reformed congregations dominate Europe and much of the northern and eastern United States. Along with the Anglican and Episcopal[75] churches, these churches trace their ancestry directly back to the Protestant Reformation, a time when many churches split off from the Roman Catholic Church for a variety of reasons.

Lutherans trace their spiritual ancestry back to Martin Luther. Conservative Lutherans continue to follow his teachings closely and literally. The more conservative Lutheran denominations are highly organized, dogmatic, and liturgical. They are extremely resistant to change, both religious and cultural. In many of these churches, dancing and other activities which are commonplace today are still prohibited.

However, the largest Lutheran denomination in the United States (the ELCA) is more liberal, accepting people of many different beliefs. They claim to follow Luther by questioning, as he did, established traditions in light of Scriptural evidence. Some pastors in this denomination even have significant Messianic leanings. However, this liberal attitude has also led many ELCA churches to accept, for example, homosexual unions.

Anglicanism, the third largest international denomination, came into its own as a separate denomination from Roman

Catholicism during the sixteenth century. However, English Christians have a unique and ancient history of their own, which has helped to inform and direct modern Anglicanism. The tension between the Catholic and Protestant streams of faith which helped shape Anglican theology and praxis has birthed a denomination with a surprisingly broad theological tent, yet which still retains a highly liturgical atmosphere and the sacramental aspects of the ancient liturgical church.

The spectrum of liberal-to-conservative is mirrored in Anglicanism just as it is in Lutheranism. For example, the Anglican Communion's official branches in the United States and Canada have come under fire for allowing homosexual unions and the ordination of practicing homosexuals. Other Anglicans have repudiated these two provinces, and conservative Anglicans are pushing for the official recognition of a more conservative expression of Anglicanism in Canada and the United States.

Reformed and Presbyterian churches rely heavily on the theology of John Calvin. As in Lutheranism and Anglicanism, these churches retain some similarities to Catholicism, but have reformed aspects with which they disagree. These churches are well known for their emphasis on predestination, a foundational plank in Calvinist theology, and their adherence more or less to the Westminster Confession of Faith. Yet again, though, the different Reformed and Presbyterian denominations have reacted differently to the onset of modernism and many have become more liberal.

Traditional Protestant churches differ according to how they have reacted to the Evangelical movement. Some churches (relatively few) in these denominations have adopted an outlook that prioritizes personal commitment to Jesus via the simple gospel message and the "sinner's prayer." In many cases, they retain a strong awareness of, and identification with, their traditional heritage; in other cases, they may not be easily distinguishable from a non-denominational church.

Several traditional Protestant denominations have come under heavy criticism for their stance on homosexuality, seen by conservative Christians as a departure from the Bible's commands and a tacit rejection of the authority of the Bible. The Episcopal Church (USA), the Evangelical Lutheran Church in America, the Presbyterian Church (USA), the United Church of Canada, and many European Reformed churches have all chosen to accept homosexual behavior.

Many people continue attending churches they may not agree with for other (i.e., social) reasons. There are also conservative denominations corresponding to each of the larger traditional denominations; Missouri Synod Lutherans and Orthodox Presbyterians, for example, strongly condemn the liberal and/or modern tendencies in the larger Protestant denominations. However, at the same time, these conservative denominations are tremendously more resistant to the Messianic message, as they tend to have a far more skeptical attitude toward change.

Traditional Protestants, especially Anglicans, generally retain some elements of Catholicism that are not present in non-denominational churches. These may include, but are not limited to, liturgical worship, "high church" architecture, top-down governmental structure (though many Reformed churches are congregational), a more formal approach to clergy and ordination, and a less symbolic, more literal view of the sacraments.

When encountering more liberal streams of Protestantism, the idea that the church can choose to depart from what the Bible teaches represents an obstacle to the *shaliach* that he will not be as likely to encounter in more conservative churches. It may be possible, though difficult, to reconnect traditional Protestants in more liberal denominations with their spiritual heritage of faith in God's revealed word.

However, the emphasis on social issues in liberal churches provides a point of commonality with the *shaliach*, as the Torah also speaks to many social issues and provides practical solutions to problems like poverty and hunger. Furthermore, the ecumenical emphasis of some of these denominations and their liberality may cause them to be more open to new ideas.

More conservative forms of Lutheranism and Presbyterianism tend to be highly resistant to change and are likely to reject anything that seems new or different. Nevertheless, these churches cannot all be lumped together and must be judged on a case-by-case basis.

CHARISMATIC CHURCHES

The worldwide charismatic movement has affected all denominations, so it is difficult to describe charismatic churches beyond what makes them distinct. The movement is quite large; there are several charismatic denominations, among them Assemblies of God and Foursquare. A large minority of non-denominational churches are also charismatic. Many denominational Christians also identify as charismatic, including over a hundred million Roman Catholics.

Charismatic Christians emphasize the work of the Holy Spirit. They may encourage or even require one to undergo an experiential baptism of the Holy Spirit, complete with charismatic manifestations such as speaking in tongues. Worship in charismatic churches is expressive, with loud vocalizations and physical expressions such as upraised hands.

Charismatic churches have been accused of replacing theology with shallow, experiential religion. However, charismatic theology is just as deep and systematic as traditional Christian theology, and there are several reputable charismatic seminaries.

Charismatic believers see themselves as restoring a New Testament form of worship; the book of Acts is central, as it portrays repeated supernatural events surrounding the work of the Holy Spirit. The term "Pentecostal," applied to many charismatic churches, refers to the outpouring of the Holy Spirit in Acts 2.

The *shaliach* can help a charismatic believer get in touch with his own foundational principles by presenting the Messianic movement as a move of the Holy Spirit—which it is and always has been. The role of the Holy Spirit in bringing people to a realization of the Torah's relevance and Israel's centrality is absolutely vital. Many believers who already sense and try to follow the leading of the Spirit have been led directly to the Messianic faith.

THE EMERGING CHURCH

The "emerging church" is a loosely (if at all) affiliated, non-denominational (and/or interdenominational) movement designed to address the perceived Western cultural shift from "modern" to "postmodern." Emerging churches are even more difficult to describe than Charismatic churches, as they have all addressed this cultural shift in different ways. They tend, though, to critique modern Evangelicalism and the culture in which it flourished.

Emerging churches generally reject concepts like absolutism, rationalism, and other hallmarks of Enlightenment thought in favor of more organic concepts like narrative and tradition (not necessarily "church tradition" as in confessions and creeds, but the idea of tradition rather than absolute truth supplying meaning, definition, and perspective to a community).

Emerging churches tend to eschew hierarchical organizational structures, taking a more communal approach to "doing church." The highly organized church service (whether modern or liturgical) is replaced with communal interaction, imagery, and authenticity.

The degree to which these values are embraced is different in different emerging churches; as these churches are even more likely to directly reflect the spirit of the community which they represent than denominational or traditionally organized churches are, it is hard to know what to expect in an emerging church.

The push for authenticity, the questioning attitude, the search for meaning, and the willingness to change are all aspects of the emerging church that the *shaliach* can connect with and affirm. However, the emerging church's reticence to accept the idea of absolute truth may make the *shaliach*'s message just one "truth" among many; he may find acceptance, but this will not necessarily correlate with an ability to affect change.

A FINAL WORD

These summaries are prohibitively short and do not really do justice to the heritage of each tradition. They represent broad generalizations that do not apply in every church or on every level. They are not designed to fully equip you, but rather, to get you started in the right direction, whichever way that might be.

It is important to remember that even within one denomination, there are significant variations. "High church" and "low church" worship can both be found in many denominations. Charismatics and Evangelicals can also be found almost everywhere, at least in the United States.

Regional differences also have an impact on how churches operate. Churches in the "Bible Belt" of the United States are more likely to be conservative than churches on the east or west coast or far to the north, regardless of denomination. Similarly, churches in rural areas tend to be both more conservative theologically and less modern in worship style than churches in the city, as things tend to change more rapidly in larger urban areas. But again, these are only generalizations.

The best way to get to know a church is to attend, listen, learn, ask questions, be interested, and be respectful.

Tools for the Shaliach

Resources to help flesh out
and communicate the gospel
of the kingdom of heaven.

F irst Fruits of Zion has spent years producing resources to help Christians understand their roots in Judaism. We feel that the following books may prove particularly useful to one who would introduce his Christian brothers and sisters to the Jewish Jesus, his people Israel, and his Torah.

BOOKS AND WORKBOOKS

RESTORATION: RETURNING THE TORAH OF GOD TO THE DISCIPLES OF JESUS

D. Thomas Lancaster addresses basic Christian objections to the Torah, explaining that it is God's revealed will for his people and not, as it has been traditionally understood, a burden. He goes through the different laws of the Torah and explains their beauty and their contemporary application. He also goes through difficult concepts like the oral Torah, and addresses objections like the accusation that keeping Torah is legalistic and that Paul taught against it.

AVAILABLE: Book, Workbook (for small groups), Audiobooks (Formats: CD and MP3)

BOUNDARY STONES

Boundary Stones presents a compelling and positive case for the Torah to return as life's guidebook for every disciple of Yeshua the Messiah. Many Christians may find Aaron Eby's simple, short, well-thought out chapters to be an appealing introduction to the concept of Torah and how it was designed to be a guide for God's people.

AVAILABLE: Book, Workbook (for small groups), Audiobooks (Formats: CD and MP3)

BOOKS

THE HOLY EPISTLE TO THE GALATIANS: SERMONS FROM A MESSIANIC JEWISH PERSPECTIVE

D. Thomas Lancaster's measured walk through Galatians can help Christians understand some of the assumptions they bring to the table as far as biblical interpretation. Lancaster goes over the social situation of the early Gentile believers and the reason for Paul's apparent polemic against the Mosaic Law in Galatians. He also explains the difference between Jews and Gentiles in a way that should alleviate the concerns of Christians who think that Messianic Gentiles are trying to proselytize them to Judaism.

GRAFTED IN: ISRAEL, GENTILES, AND THE MYSTERY OF THE GOSPEL

Paul's passage in Romans 11 about being "grafted in" is a seminal text for exploring the role and identity of Gentile believers, their relationship with Israel, and their standing before God. D. Thomas Lancaster's exploration of these concepts will be a helpful supplement to the Christian who would be willing to consider the election of the Jewish people but is not sure how he would then fit into God's redemptive plan as a Gentile.

GOD-FEARERS: GENTILES & THE GOD OF ISRAEL

God-Fearers looks at the historical connection that non-Jews had with the people of Israel. This resource attempts to demonstrate how Gentiles can connect to Israel, the Jewish people, and the Torah in a healthy and balanced manner. Toby Janicki works through, with the reader, concepts and viewpoints on the multiple applications of the Torah, the Apostolic mandates on Gentile's coming to faith, and more. This book will bring balance, affirmation, and form a biblically structured approach to the commandments for Gentiles.

AVAILABLE: Book, Audiobooks (Formats: CD and MP3)

ADVANCED RESOURCES

HAYESOD: THE FOUNDATION

HaYesod is a complete discipleship course that respectfully explores the Jewish foundation of Christianity. Comprehensive workbooks, lesson guides, and additional supplementary materials make this program one of the most well-rounded and comprehensive studies of this area of biblical studies. Christians who have some level of exposure to the Messianic movement and who are truly interested in developing their knowledge of the Jewish roots of their faith would really benefit from going through HaYesod. Visit www.hayesod.org for more information.

APPLICATION: The HaYesod program is a 10-lesson intensive course on the Jewish roots of Christianity. It focuses on educating Christians in their relationship to the Land, the People, and the Scriptures of Israel. The lectures are professionally produced on DVD and the students follow along in comprehensive workbooks. This class is a great introduction that will challenge and spark discussion.

TORAH CLUB

Torah Club is a First Fruits of Zion flagship six-volume commentary on the Torah, the Haftarot, the New Testament, and the history of Christianity through the first century. This comprehensive resource provides materials for years of in-depth study for those who want to experience the entire Bible from a Messianic perspective.

APPLICATION: Torah Club can be used in a variety of ways. It is perfect for small group studies and Sunday school programs. The multiple volumes allow for years of study on various levels of interest. These volumes take students through the entire Torah, the Prophets, Gospels, Epistles and even progress through early church history. The lessons are weekly and span over the course of one year. Visit www.torahclub.org for more information. Here is a summary of each volume.

VOLUME 1: UNROLLING THE SCROLL

This is Torah 101 for everyone, introducing students to both the Jewish roots of Christianity and the world of Messianic Judaism. More than just a weekly reading guide or Bible commentary, *Volume One* is filled with new insights and practical implications which exhort us to practice righteousness while developing a deeper relationship with our Father in Heaven.

WRITTEN COMMENTARY: 928 pages

AUDIO MAGAZINE: 30 hours on 27 CDs

VOLUME 2: SHADOWS OF THE MESSIAH

Find the Messiah in places you never expected as you discover him through the Five Books of Moses according to the weekly Bible portions read in synagogues. *Volume Two* is like walking the Emmaus Road with the Master himself where "beginning with Moses and with all the prophets, he explained to them the things concerning himself in all the Scriptures" (Luke 24:27).

WRITTEN COMMENTARY: 838 pages

AUDIO MAGAZINE: 29 hours on 27 CDs

VOLUME 3: VOICE OF THE PROPHETS

Dive deep into the world of ancient Israel, kings and prophets. Enter the world of Isaiah, Jeremiah, and Ezekiel. Study prophecies about the end of days. *Volume Three* takes students through the synagogue haftarah readings—the section from the Prophets that accompanies the weekly Torah portion.

WRITTEN COMMENTARY: 1,256 pages

AUDIO MAGAZINE: 34 hours on 27 CDs

VOLUME 4: CHRONICLES OF THE MESSIAH

Messianic commentary on a harmonized, narrative approach to the four Gospels. *Volume Four* presents the Gospel story in its historical and Jewish context; unravel the difficult words and parables of the Master; study rabbinic parallels to the Gospel teachings and discover the lost Gospel message and call to discipleship.

WRITTEN COMMENTARY: 1,536 pages

AUDIO MAGAZINE: 28 hours on 27 CDs

VOLUME 5: DEPTHS OF THE TORAH

Study biblical poetry, narrative form, midrash, and New Testament interpretation with a literary approach to Torah study. Examine apostolic interpretations of Torah and compare with the rabbinic thought. Devotional, inspirational, and unapologetically Messiah-centered, *Volume Five* offers practical direction for Torah-living.

WRITTEN COMMENTARY: 1,228 pages

AUDIO MAGAZINE: 28 hours on 27 CDs

VOLUME 6: CHRONICLES OF THE APOSTLES

Follow the lives and adventures of the apostles through the book of Acts and into the lost chapter of church history. Study Jewish sources, church fathers, and Christian history to reveal the untold story of the disciples into the second century. *Volume Six* presents a revolutionary look at the book of Acts with Messianic commentary and Jewish insights into the Epistles.

WRITTEN COMMENTARY: 1,400 pages

AUDIO MAGAZINE: 28 hours on 27 CDs

Bibliography

Bacchiocchi, Samuele. *From Sabbath to Sunday.* Rome: The Pontifical Gregorian University Press, 1977.

Bockmuehl, Marcus. "God's Life as a Jew: Remembering the Son of God as Son of David." In *Seeking the Identity of Jesus: A Pilgrimage.* Edited by Beverly Roberts Gaventa and Richard B. Hays. Grand Rapids: Eerdmans, 2008: 60–78.

Dauermann, Stuart. *Son of David: Healing the Vision of the Messianic Jewish Movement.* Eugene, OR: Wipf & Stock, 2010.

Eby, Aaron. *Biblically Kosher: A Messianic Jewish Perspective on Kashrut.* Marshfield, MO: First Fruits of Zion, 2012.

Fishkoff, Sue. *The Rebbe's Army.* New York: Schocken, 2003.

Fredricksen, Paula. "What 'Parting of the Ways'? Jews, Gentiles, and the Ancient Mediterranean City." In *The Ways that Never Parted: Jews and Christians in Late Antiquity and the Early Middle Ages.* Edited by Adam H. Becker and Annette Yoshiko Reed. Tübingen: Mohr Siebeck, 2003: 35–63.

Gillet, Lev. *Communion in the Messiah.* Cambridge: James Clarke & Co., 1942.

Herczeg, Israel Isser Zvi. *The Torah with Rashi's Commentary Translated, Annotated, and Elucidated*, vol. 3, *Vayikra.* Brooklyn: Artscroll, 1994.

Hislop, Alexander. *The Two Babylons.* Self-published in 1853.

Janicki, Toby. *God-Fearers: Gentiles and the God of Israel.* Marshfield, MO: First Fruits of Zion, 2012.

Lancaster, D. Thomas. *King of the Jews.* Littleton, CO: First Fruits of Zion, 2006.

Lancaster, D. Thomas. "This Man Breaks the Sabbath, part 1." *Messiah Journal* 104 (Summer 2010): 16–33.

Lancaster, D. Thomas. "This Man Breaks the Sabbath, part 2." *Messiah Journal* 106 (Spring 2011): 26–43.

Lancaster, D. Thomas. *The Holy Epistle to the Galatians: Sermons from a Messianic Jewish Perspective.* Marshfield, MO: First Fruits of Zion, 2011.

Levertoff, Paul Philip. *Love and the Messianic Age.* Marshfield, MO: Vine of David, 2009.

McKnight, Scot. *The King Jesus Gospel.* Grand Rapids: Zondervan, 2011.

Michael, Boaz, and D. Thomas Lancaster. "One Law and the Messianic Gentile." *Messiah Journal* 101 (Summer 2009): 46–75.

Michael, Boaz. *Twelve Gates: Where Do the Nations Enter?* Marshfield, MO: First Fruits of Zion, 2012.

Miller, Zvi. *Thirty Days to Teshuvah.* Southfield: Targum Press, 2005.

Nanos, Mark. *The Mystery of Romans: The Jewish Context of Paul's Letter.* Minneapolis: Fortress, 1996.

Noble, Perry. "Eight Ways to Tell That I Might Be a Pharisee." No pages. Cited 7 May 2012. Online: http://www.christianpost.com/news/eight-ways-to-tell-that-i-might-be-a-pharisee-74358/.

Notley, R. Steven, and Ze'ev Safrai. *Parables of the Sages: Jewish Wisdom from Jesus to Rav Ashi.* Jerusalem: Carta, 2011.

Roberts, Alexander, and James Donaldson. *The Ante-Nicene Fathers.* 10 vols. Grand Rapids: Eerdmans, 1950–51.

Rudolph, David. "Messianic Jews and Christian Theology: Restoring an Historical Voice to the Contemporary Discussion." *Pro Ecclesia* XIV no. 1 (2005): 58–84.

Rudolph, David. "The Celebration of Passover by Gentile Christians in the Patristic Period." *Messiah Journal* 107 (Spring 2011): 57–58.

Rudolph, David. *A Jew to the Jews: Jewish Contours of Pauline Flexibility in 1 Corinthians 9:19–23.* Tübingen: Mohr Siebeck, 2011.

Soulen, R. Kendall. *The God of Israel and Christian Theology.* Minneapolis: Fortress, 1996.

Stackhouse, John G., Jr., ed. *What Does It Mean To Be Saved?* Grand Rapids: Baker Academic, 2002.

Stendahl, Krister. "The Apostle Paul and the Introspective Conscience of the West." In *Paul Among Jews and Gentiles.* Minneapolis: Fortress, 1976: 78–96.

Tverberg, Lois, and Ann Spangler. *Sitting at the Feet of Rabbi Jesus.* Grand Rapids: Zondervan, 2009.

Tverberg, Lois. *Walking in the Dust of Rabbi Jesus.* Grand Rapids: Zondervan, 2012.

Tucker, Brian. *Remain in Your Calling: Paul and the Continuation of Social Identities in 1 Corinthians.* Eugene, OR: Pickwick Publications, 2011.

Viola, Frank, and George Barna. *Pagan Christianity?: Exploring the Roots of Our Church Practices.* Wheaton, IL: Tyndale, 2008.

Wright, N. T. *Hebrews for Everyone.* Louisville: Westminster John Knox Press, 2004.

Wright, N. T. *Justification.* Downers Grove, IL: InterVarsity, 2009.

Young, Brad. *Jesus the Jewish Theologian.* Grand Rapids: Baker, 1993.

Young, Brad. *The Parables: Jewish Tradition and Christian Interpretation.* Grand Rapids: Baker, 2008.

Zetterholm, Magnus. *The Formation of Christianity in Antioch: A Social-Scientific Approach to the Separation between Judaism and Christianity.* New York: Routledge, 2003.

Endnotes

1   David Rudolph, "Messianic Jews and Christian Theology:
     Restoring an Historical Voice to the Contemporary Discussion,"
     Pro Ecclesia XIV no. 1 (2005): 83. Some believe that the
     disappearance of Jewish Christianity is evidence that Yeshua is
     not the Messiah. Hand in hand with this belief is the idea that
     Christianity is not a legitimate religion. This is the traditional
     Jewish view. This book is not designed to address this concern.
     However, the reappearance of Messianic Judaism in our time,
     along with the waves of Gentiles who are moving to take on the
     commandments of Torah and rediscover a Biblical theology of
     Israel and the Jewish people, are evidence to me that God's hand
     has been at work throughout history to accomplish exactly what he
     intended. "It is not as though God's word had failed" (Romans 9:6).

2   Mark Nanos, *The Mystery of Romans* (Minneapolis: Fortress, 1996),
     166–238.

3   Eugene, OR: Wipf & Stock, 2010.

4   Dauermann, 2.

5   R. Kendall Soulen, *The God of Israel and Christian Theology*
     (Minneapolis: Fortress, 1996), 130, emphasis in original.

6   I distinguish between the Messianic Jewish movement, which
     consists of the formal institutions of Messianic Judaism as
     represented by solid, grounded, Jewish denominations and
     synagogues, and the Hebrew roots movement, a loosely organized
     group of Gentiles who are exploring and embracing the Jewish
     roots of their faith in Messiah.

7   It is not my intention in this book to recount all of the historic
     failings of institutional Christianity. One could rightly point
     out that in many times and places, Christianity became the
     dominant religion by force, by the sword. Representatives of the
     Christian church have at times murdered, stolen, and lied their
     way to the top. They have married clerical power with political
     power, resulting at times in a cultural Christianity that is devoid
     of real commitment. However, I do not believe that these people

are representative of average Christians today, who is just trying to live a life of faith, and balance their beliefs with the rest of the pressures that confront people on a daily basis. Here I am dealing with the average Christian, not so much "the church" as the church down the street, full of regular people who are trying to do something good.

8   This notion has even had some degree of scholarly support, in the *Religionsgeschichtliche Schule* and the works of Rudolf Bultmann.

9   Wheaton, IL: Tyndale, 2008.

10   In fact Viola deprecates the institution of the synagogue on p. 51, n. 4, claiming it too has pagan origins!

11   *From Sabbath to Sunday* (Rome: The Pontifical Gregorian University Press, 1977).

12   In his 1539 treatise, "Against the Antinomians."

13   Aaron Eby, *Biblically Kosher* (Marshfield, MO: First Fruits of Zion, 2012), gives many examples of how rejection of Jewish traditional interpretation of the dietary laws actually often cloaks a rejection of many of the dietary laws themselves, such as the removal of the sciatic nerve, the removal of blood by salting, and the separation of meat and dairy, all of which have firm roots in the text of the Torah, and without all of which someone cannot be said to "keep kosher."

14   Toby Janicki discusses which dietary laws the apostles laid on Gentiles in *God-Fearers* (Marshfield, MO: First Fruits of Zion, 2012), 55–57.

15   *Communion in the Messiah* (Cambridge: James Clarke & Co., 1942), 73.

16   Many of the Rambam's statements on Christianity were censored by the medieval church and are not as widely known or accepted.

17   *Satī* was the practice of immolating women on their husbands' funeral pyres.

18   R. Kendall Soulen, *The God of Israel and Christian Theology* (Minneapolis: Fortress, 1996), 137.

19   Grand Rapids: Zondervan, 2011.

20   N.T. Wright, *Justification* (Downers Grove, IL: InterVarsity, 2009).

21   "God's Life as a Jew: Remembering the Son of God as Son of
     David," in *Seeking the Identity of Jesus: A Pilgrimage* (ed. Beverly
     Roberts Gaventa and Richard B. Hays; Grand Rapids: Eerdmans,
     2008), 77.

22   Dauermann, 3.

23   D. Thomas Lancaster, Torah Club Volume 4, *Terumah*, 486; R.
     Steven Notley and Ze'ev Safrai, *Parables of the Sages: Jewish Wisdom
     from Jesus to Rav Ashi* (Jerusalem: Carta, 2011), 28–31.

24   N.T. Wright, *Hebrews for Everyone* (Louisville: Westminster
     John Knox Press, 2004), 89, states that at the end of the Second
     Temple Period, the followers of Yeshua believed that "the previous
     covenant, Temple, priesthood, and all, [were] 'out of date' and
     'about to disappear.'"

25   Yeshua would have observed these laws according to the *halacha*
     as it was developed in his time. Of course, we cannot project later
     halachic developments back into Yeshua's time.

26   *Jesus the Jewish Theologian* (Grand Rapids: Baker, 1993) and *The
     Parables: Jewish Tradition and Christian Interpretation* (Grand
     Rapids: Baker, 2008), among others.

27   *Sitting at the Feet of Rabbi Jesus* (Grand Rapids: Zondervan, 2009)
     and *Walking in the Dust of Rabbi Jesus* (Grand Rapids: Zondervan,
     2012).

28   D. Thomas Lancaster, *King of the Jews* (Littleton, CO: First Fruits of
     Zion, 2006), in addition to Torah Club Volume Four, the Delitzsch
     Hebrew Gospels, and several other relevant works.

29   All of these are alluded to or described in Luke 2.

30   Luke 4:16.

31   Mark 7:25–29, Matthew 10:5.

32   Mark 9:5, 10:51, 11:21; John 1:38, 1:49, 3:2, 3:26, 6:25, 9:2, 11:8.

33   Matthew 26; Mark 14; Luke 22; John 6:4, 11:55, and ch. 13.

34   John 10:22.

35   John 7.

36   "What 'Parting of the Ways'? Jews, Gentiles, and the Ancient
     Mediterranean City," in *The Ways that Never Parted: Jews and*

Christians in Late Antiquity and the Early Middle Ages (ed. Adam H. Becker and Annette Yoshiko Reed; Tübingen: Mohr Siebeck, 2003), 35–63.

37 *Mystery of Romans*, 10.

38 "Dialogue with Trypho," in *The Ante-Nicene Fathers* (ed. Alexander Roberts and James Donaldson; Grand Rapids: Eerdmans, 1950–51), 1:200.

39 *The Formation of Christianity in Antioch: A Social-Scientific Approach to the Separation between Judaism and Christianity* (New York: Routledge, 2003).

40 Western Christians moved to a Sunday observance earlier, after the Second Jewish War in 135 CE. See David Rudolph, "The Celebration of Passover by Gentile Christians in the Patristic Period," in *Messiah Journal* 107 (Spring 2011): 57–58.

41 In *Paul Among Jews and Gentiles* (Minneapolis: Fortress, 1976), 78–96. Modern academic views on Paul as a Torah-observant Jew can usually trace their roots directly back to Stendahl's work.

42 Janicki, *God-Fearers*, 80. This is just one example; throughout the entire book, Toby has laid out a comprehensive theology of Gentile identity in the body of Christ.

43 McKnight, 30.

44 Janicki, *God-Fearers*, 49–72.

45 The Greek word usually translated "church" in the New Testament.

46 John G. Stackhouse, Jr., ed., *What Does It Mean to Be Saved?* (Grand Rapids: Baker Academic, 2002), 9–10.

47 Incidentally, this is where the similarities end; other Gnostic beliefs, such as the creation of the world by a demiurge, the repudiation of the physical realm as inherently evil, and the belief that Jesus did not come in a real human body were not adopted by Christianity.

48 McKnight, *King Jesus Gospel*, 25–26.

49 Lancaster, Torah Club Volume 4, *Toldot*, 134.

50 Paul Philip Levertoff, *Love and the Messianic Age* (Marshfield, MO: Vine of David, 2009), 32.

51   m.*Berachot* 5.5.

52   Sometimes this claim is made under the impression that Gentile
      believers are descended from the lost tribes of Israel, a concept that
      is explored in my recent book, *Twelve Gates: Where Do the Nations
      Enter?* (Marshfield, MO: First Fruits of Zion, 2012).

53   Daniel Lancaster, "This Man Breaks the Sabbath," part 1 in *Messiah
      Journal* 104 (Summer 2010): 16–33, and part 2 in *Messiah Journal* 106
      (Spring 2011): 26–43, demonstrates how Yeshua kept the Sabbath
      according to *halacha*, including the restrictions of the thirty-nine
      melachot, and found halachic justification for the actions he took
      on the Sabbath. The New Testament therefore indicates that
      keeping the Sabbath is much more than just not working, or going
      to synagogue—to be kept, it must be kept within traditional Jewish
      guidelines.

54   John 5:39; Romans 10:4; 2 Corinthians 3:7ff.; Galatians 3:23–29;
      Colossians 2:17; Hebrews 1:1–2, 3:1–6.

55   See for example *Likkutei Sichot*, vol. 21, *hosafot Shemot*; *Midrash
      Tanchuma*, *Toldot* 14, among other sources.

56   For more on this topic, see my book, *Twelve Gates*.

57   On Galatians specifically see D. Thomas Lancaster, *The Holy
      Epistle to the Galatians: Sermons from a Messianic Jewish Perspective*
      (Marshfield, MO: First Fruits of Zion, 2011).

58   Toby Janicki, *God-Fearers*, 39–47. The rest of *God-Fearers* is also
      informative in developing a coherent identity as a believing
      Gentile, as well as chapter four of *Twelve Gates*.

59   Tübingen: Mohr Siebeck, 2011.

60   New York: Schocken, 2003.

61   This section was inspired by Perry Noble's unfortunately titled
      essay, "Eight Ways to Tell That I Might Be a Pharisee," n.p. [cited
      7 May 2012]. Online: http://www.christianpost.com/news/eight-
      ways-to-tell-that-i-might-be-a-pharisee-74358/.

62   2 Corinthians 4:5–12.

63   Matthew 5:3–12.

64   Romans 12:10.

65   Matthew 9:9–13.

66   Matthew 7:1–5.

67   Zvi Miller, *Thirty Days to Teshuvah* (Southfield: Targum Press, 2005), 74.

68   For a fuller exploration of this idea, see my article with D. Thomas Lancaster, "One Law and the Messianic Gentile," in *Messiah Journal* 101 (Summer 2009): 46–75.

69   Toby Janicki details which commandments these are in *God-Fearers*, 49–72.

70   Israel Yisser Zvi Herczeg, *The Torah with Rashi's Commentary Translated, Annotated, and Elucidated*, vol. 3, *Vayikra* (Brooklyn: Artscroll, 1994), 235.

71   In fact, it is common for Messianic Jews to connect the bread and wine of the Last Supper with the weekly kiddush, the blessing which brings in the Sabbath day and which also involves bread and wine. This token observance is not explicitly commanded by Yeshua, but there is nothing wrong with it. Similarly, Yeshua didn't command his disciples to celebrate the Lord's Supper on Sunday morning, but this doesn't make it a violation of his commandments to do so.

72   *Love and the Messianic Age*, 24.

73   Jim Collins, *Good to Great* (New York: HarperCollins, 2001), 1.

74   *Catechism of the Catholic Church*, paragraph 1324.

75   Anglicans differ as to whether they should be called Protestant or Catholic, and depending on how the terms are used, many Anglicans identify with both. While they are not "Roman Catholic," Anglicans see themselves as part of a continuous stream—the "catholic" (universal) church—which goes back to the church's inception. However, like other Protestant denominations, the Anglican Church broke from the Roman Catholic Church over various issues.